CULTURE SHOCK!

Finland

Deborah Swallow

Graphic Arts Center Publishing Company
Portland, Oregon

In the same series

Argentina	*Egypt*	*Korea*	*Spain*
Australia	*Finland*	*Laos*	*Sri Lanka*
Austria	*France*	*Malaysia*	*Sweden*
Bolivia	*Germany*	*Mauritius*	*Switzerland*
Borneo	*Greece*	*Mexico*	*Syria*
Britain	*Hong Kong*	*Morocco*	*Taiwan*
Burma	*Hungary*	*Myanmar*	*Thailand*
California	*India*	*Nepal*	*Turkey*
Canada	*Indonesia*	*Netherlands*	*UAE*
Chile	*Iran*	*Norway*	*Ukraine*
China	*Ireland*	*Pakistan*	*USA*
Cuba	*Israel*	*Philippines*	*USA—The South*
Czech Republic	*Italy*	*Singapore*	*Venezuela*
Denmark	*Japan*	*South Africa*	*Vietnam*

Barcelona At Your Door	*Paris At Your Door*	*A Traveller's Medical*
Chicago At Your Door	*Rome At Your Door*	*Guide*
Havana At Your Door	*San Francisco At Your*	*A Wife's Guide*
Jakarta At Your Door	*Door*	*Living and Working*
Kuala Lumpur, Malaysia		*Abroad*
At Your Door	*A Globe-Trotter's Guide*	*Working Holidays*
London At Your Door	*A Parent's Guide*	*Abroad*
New York At Your Door	*A Student's Guide*	

Illustrations by TRIGG
Photographs by Deborah Swallow; with the exception of those on pp. 58, 99, 112, 119 and 160 which are courtesy of the Finnish Tourist Board, UK Office.

© 2001 Times Media Private Limited

This book is published by special
arrangement with Times Media Private Limited
Times Centre, 1 New Industrial Road, Singapore 536196
International Standard Book Number 1-55868-592-8
Library of Congress Card Number: 00-110097

Graphic Arts Center Publishing Company
P.O. Box 10306 • Portland, Oregon 97296-0306 • (503) 226-2402

Printed in Singapore

CONTENTS

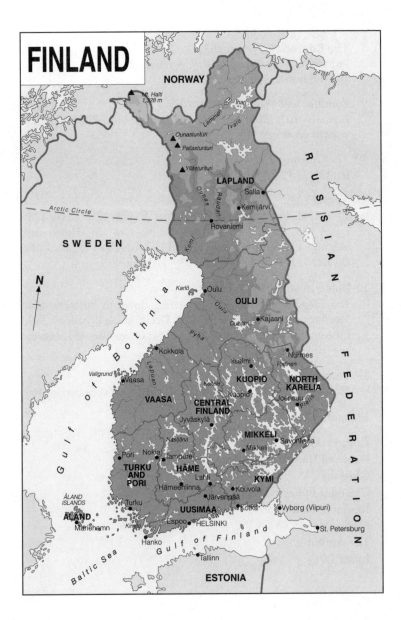

PREFACE

I first fell in love with Finland in the summer of 1997. It was my first trip to the country and I was travelling with my new boss, Seppo, who was Finnish. He spent the entire plane trip from Heathrow Airport, London, to Helsinki enthusing about his country, telling me about the people and the geography. It was obvious he had such a love and a pride for Finland. Since then, I've been travelling to Finland at least once or twice every month and his enthusiasm and love for his country has spilled over to me. I now realise, of course, that this love and pride is not exclusive to Seppo, but is shared by the Finns as a race.

Indeed, this love and pride is well deserved. This small nation has made a substantial contribution to world civilisation out of proportion to its size and the number of its population. Finland is not a major power; neither is it along any main routes, so few people really get to know the country.

The lakes of Central Finland

In 1990, Finland was thought to be the most expensive country in the world. However, today it is far more affordable, especially when compared with its Scandinavian neighbours. The Finns currently enjoy more prosperity than their counterparts in most of the developed industrial counties, but they have a more peaceful lifestyle and live in a 'softer' society.

Finland is a land full of contrasts and contradictions. The Finns themselves often seem aloof or restrained but in contrast, once you get to know them, you will find that they have a great sense of humour (and can be very noisy!). Of course the weather in the winter can be extremely cold, but that first summer I spent in Finland the temperature was more than 30°C. The long winter nights are contrasted with the wonderfully long summer days of sunshine. Over the years, both East and West have influenced Finland and, therefore, its culture is a surprising mixture of the two. Some of the old traditions of the East survive happily in a high-tech world. The Finns themselves love new and modern things, and always have the latest gadgets, but in stark contrast some of their customs have their roots in a bygone age.

Finland is a country where you can still get away from it all. It is full of undisturbed forests, crystal-clear lakes and huge quiet skies. But when you've had enough of the peace and quiet you can roll into town and enjoy the many activities going on. There are always festivals and concerts taking place and a town never misses out on its weekly dances!

It has been said that the Finns are very dour and solemn. But they do enjoy a good laugh and have a great sense of humour. They are the first to joke about themselves and have a great sense of humility: *"An American, a German and a Finn are looking at an elephant. The American wonders if the elephant would be good in a circus, the German wonders what price he would get if he sold it, and the Finn asks himself, 'I wonder what the elephant thinks of me?'"* I hope as the reader you will find this an informative book about Finland, but my main wish is to help you understand some of those things that have captivated, delighted, charmed and sometimes puzzled me about this country. Finns argue that they are extremely individualistic, although, to the outside world, they share a group mentality and dislike standing out in the crowd.

This book is not meant to be the definitive tourist guide; there are plenty of those. Therefore, the reader will find in this book only brief descriptions of the regions and tourist centres. What this book tries to do is paint a picture of Finnish life, as seen through my eyes and heard through my ears, and drawing on Finnish history to explain its culture, its traditions, its behaviour, its literature, music and mindset. As one brought up in an overpopulated part of southeast England, of English parents, and with a British cultural background, my interpretation of Finnish life is, therefore, coloured by my own background. However, I hope that I have been able to intertwine with my own thoughts the many stories and various experiences of foreign colleagues, friends and fellow travellers that I have met along the way.

Finland is a highly industrialised nation with a deep-rooted sense of time-honoured values. In many respects, it has protected itself from the greed of individuals and has worked towards the common good. I believe that I have been privileged to experience a gentle sort of society at the end of a violent, war-torn twentieth century. Now poised at the beginning of a new millennium, one has to wonder how much Finland will change as it takes its rightful, prominent place on the world stage.

ACKNOWLEDGMENTS

To my colleagues and fellow travellers whose shared stories have helped make Finland such a colourful place. To Mitzi for her invaluable help in creating the first draft. To PKP whose tips, hints and efficiency were a constant source of enlightenment and of great practical use in the writing and editing of this book. To Mia at the Finnish Tourist Board in London who 'came up trumps' just when I needed some help. And ... to my family whose patience has lasted somewhat longer than we first anticipated! Thank you.

– Chapter One –

FINLAND: A LAND FOR ALL SEASONS

Very few people know where Finland actually is. Everyone has heard of the country, but few can pinpoint it on a map. Most people associate it with Scandinavia, saying, "It's somewhere up there." I was one of those people. For my first trip to Finland, in great excitement, I got out our big family world atlas. I turned to the pages for the Nordic countries and eagerly sought the town which I was visiting in Finland. To my absolute consternation, I found that Finland was well north of Moscow. I never thought that there was much north of Moscow. I found Kuopio, the town that I was visiting, was so far north that the only three towns that I recognised on the map north of there were the Russian towns of Archangel and Murmansk, and Reykjavik in Iceland! I thought I was going to the North Pole.

How wrong I was.

Finland is not officially part of Scandinavia. It is one of the Nordic countries and is referred to sometimes as one of the Baltic States. People usually go to Finland because they have a reason to, not because it is a convenient stopover. Finland has never been on the main route to anywhere. However, this has recently changed as the Japanese are now finding that the capital city, Helsinki, is a great place to stop on their way to the rest of Europe. Nowadays, the quickest routes into the interior of Russia are through the southern part of Finland by rail or road, as there is only one border to cross.

Although Finland has immense physical beauty, it is the people that make it memorable. Their traditions make it interesting, their love of all things modern makes it astonishing. Their language makes it impossible, and the influences from both East and West could be said to make Helsinki the 'Istanbul of the North'. Set on the Baltic, Finland's capital, Helsinki, is an intriguing mix of European, Scandinavian and Russian cultures. There are two official languages, Finnish and Swedish. In northern Finland lies the country of Lapland, home to about six thousand five hundred Sami (Lapps) who have their own language and culture.

Kuopio city centre

Contradictions and contrasts are the two words that I constantly use when describing Finland:

- The stillness of the summer forests interrupted by mosquitoes and other pesky insects in June and July.
- The absolute quiet and silence of the countryside challenged by nightlife in the city.
- The glow of the long 'white nights' in midsummer contrasted with the awesome silence of the snow-covered forests in midwinter.
- Modern versus old traditions.
- The blue, blue spring skies which contradict the complete 'white outs' in winter.
- Traditional Lapland versus cosmopolitan Helsinki.
- Vast uninterrupted forests which are actually managed.
- A well ordered country that looks totally natural.

Kuopio town square

GEOGRAPHY

Finland lies at the most eastern part of Europe and is, therefore, two hours ahead of GMT (Greenwich Mean Time). It is Europe's fifth largest country, covering 338,000 square kilometres (130,558 square miles). About 70% of the land is covered by forest, 10% is under water, and only some 6% of its total land is used for agricultural purposes, with barley and oats the main crops.

Finland is a country of considerable wilderness. There are vast areas of uninterrupted forests and woodlands, with tens of thousands of square kilometres of untouched terrain. There are more lakes in Finland than in any other country in the world.

The lakeland area of the country is an immense tangle of lakes, inlets, islands and peninsulas. There are some 187,888 lakes; 5,100 rapids; 179,584 islands and although the Finns can't name them all, they are very proud to tell you how many there are. The largest Finnish lake system, greater Saimaa, is 4,400 square kilometres wide and has some 13,710 islands. Finland is often called the Land of a Thousand Lakes. Most of these were catalogued by an engineer called Toivo Virkkala, who spent his holidays charting the waters. He started in the mid 1930s and by 1956 had managed to catalogue 1,500 lakes. (There are slightly more than 30,000 persons whose surname is Jarvinen meaning Lake Person.) Almost all Finnish municipalities have a lake, and some municipalities have more water than land in them.

To enjoy the unique beauty of this natural environment, you really do need to behave like a Finn for a while. Finns regularly take a walk in the woods in search of wild mushrooms or go berry-picking. It is a part of their way of life. From early childhood, they have become used to living in close harmony with their rich natural surroundings. These people have a respect for this priceless and irreplaceable gift, and believe it is the only way to enjoy a real relationship with the environment in which they live. The Finns have a great love of fishing, whether it is from the shores of a lake in summer, or from holes in the two-foot deep ice of a frozen lake, in the middle of winter. Whatever you are doing, it will take place in a silence that is broken only by the twittering of birds. The best way to discover Finland and the quiet beauty of this unspoiled natural environment is either on foot or by bicycle. However, it is said that the best way to see Finland is to see it from an aeroplane, as there are so few mountains or tall hills from which you can gaze out over these wondrous landscapes. Because there are no hills to interrupt the view in many parts of the country, the sky seems enormous and on fine days, in summer or winter, the blue of the sky seems to go on forever. In the south, the gentle rolling farmland slips into the vast forests and lakes of central Finland, and these gradually transform into the peat and tundra of Lapland in the north.

Virtually the whole of the country is accessible because of the hard work of the Finns in opening up remote areas. Sound Finnish engineering, in the form of good railways and road systems, has crisscrossed the forests and traversed the lakes. Endless roads run through tall trees of pine, spruce and birch. The natural barrier of thousands of lakes, which form the largest expanse of inland water in the world, has been overcome.

A river cruise boat

Nearly one-third of the country of Finland lies north of the Arctic Circle and here is where the real beauty of Lapland can be found. The semi-domesticated herds of reindeer roam freely and the remoteness of each farm makes the land seem immense. In summer, this is the land of the midnight sun and during the awesome silence of the snow-covered winter, the *aurora borealis* can be seen. The highest hills of Finland, *tunturi*, are located in Lapland, with the highest point, Halti. However, Halti, in the northwest corner of Finland is only 1,328 metres high.

Finland has borders with three countries. The border with Russia lies to the east and is 1,269 kilometres long. To the far north, Lapland has 727 kilometres of border with Norway, whilst the west of the country has a 586-kilometre border with Sweden. The Gulf of Finland separates southern Finland from Estonia. The southernmost point, Hanko, is on the same latitude as Oslo in Norway, and Anchorage in Alaska. Joensuu, in the east, is nearly as far east as Istanbul.

The landscape looks idyllic. Unfortunately, the pristine lakes are not as clean as they appear. The 1997 survey of Finland's lakes and ocean waters showed them to be some of the most polluted in the European Union (EU), failing to meet even EU minimum standards of cleanliness. This has been caused by massive pollution through paper and pulp factories, and agriculture. This pollution is the main topic of environmental debate and is a hot political issue.

Wildlife in Finland is rich and abundant. There are about 120,000 elks; Karelia, in the east, has a bear population of 240; reindeer are plentiful; along with these the animal kingdom includes the fox, lynx, wolf and wolverine. There are also 400 species of birds, including black grouse, whooper swans, osprey, black woodpeckers, chaffinches and sparrows, along with eagles and owls. Near Oulu, in the north-west of Finland, can be found one of Europe's most treasured wildlife sanctuaries, Liminganlahti. It was here, in just one week, that 300 different species of birds were recorded arriving in the spring of 2000.

CLIMATE

I think the climate was my greatest surprise when I visited Finland. It wasn't at all how I thought it would be. Most of us have a perception of long dark days in the middle of winter and Finland being so very, very cold. And yes, Finland is like that. But, the surprising thing is that it can also be so very, very hot. I am used to Mediterranean countries, where the heat of the day dies down, and becomes a warm and refreshing evening. In Finland, this does not happen, and that was my greatest surprise. As I mentioned before, on my first visit to Finland, it was experiencing a heat wave. When I woke up in the morning, it was already very warm and humid.

Naturally I thought that in the evening the temperature would drop substantially. This didn't happen, and the temperature at 8:00 p.m. was very similar to what it had been at midday. In fact, the temperature may only fall 2°C or 3°C overnight. The reason for this is the sun never goes down, so the temperature doesn't either! Until you experience this, you can have no concept of it. However, during bad weather in the summer the nights can be cool!

Enjoying summer down by Kuopio harbour

–17°C at midday!

Finland enjoys four distinct seasons. March heralds spring, when the days are becoming longer. In fact, by mid March the length of the day is longer than that in the UK. After 21 March, week by week, Finland steals a march on the rest of Europe by gaining many more hours of daylight. By the end of the month, it easily experiences fourteen hours of daylight between sun up and sun down. These are the first days of spring. Although the days are longer and can be full of sunshine, the snow can still be knee deep! But with the sunshine everything seems brighter and whiter and the promise of summer lies ahead. April sees the days lengthen from 5:30 a.m. to 10:00 p.m. By May, the snow has disappeared. The days are long, but everywhere is still brown. There are no leaves on the trees and the grass is still dead, but the forests are filled with the first flowers of the year; a small white flower like snowdrops. Everything is awaiting the new summer growth which will start towards the end of the month. The length of the day has stretched to nineteen hours.

In the far north of Finland, from mid May until late July there is continual daylight. This is the land of the midnight sun. In Rovaniemi, on the Arctic Circle, the midnight sun lasts from 20 May until 20 July. This means there is continual daylight because the sun is forever above the horizon. In central and southern Finland, 'officially' there is no midnight sun because the sun does dip just below the horizon. However, the night never really grows dark. It is just dusk for an hour and a half. At this time, the sky will take on the most beautiful hues. To you and me, this is the midnight sun and the experience is truly awe-inspiring…breathtaking…unbelievable.

In June, the leaves are out and the grass is green. Rhododendrons blossom and wither quickly, followed in quick succession by a multitude of different blooms. Window boxes are full of geraniums, bizzie lizzies, and numerous other colourful flowers. As the days become ever longer, the richness and vibrancy of Finland's slumbering beauty burst upon the landscape, accompanied by those skittish sorts of days I remember as a child in England.

Compared with Siberia, Greenland and Alaska, the Finnish climate is relatively warm. This is due to the warming effect of the Baltic Sea and the winds from the Gulf Stream. In summer you can experience hot spells, around 28°C to 30°C. However, the temperature can be as low as 10°C at times. When the weather is hot, it is, of course, very humid. The weather is very unstable in Finland and you can never tell from one day to the next what the weather will be like. Therefore, it is always advisable to have a raincoat and cardigan with you.

There is a Finnish saying about how long it will be until the summer starts, *"One month from sighting a skylark, half a month from a chaffinch, just a little from a white wagtail and not a single day from a swift."*

By mid-August the days are already beginning to be noticeably shorter. No longer does the evening twilight merge straight into the half-light of morning. By the beginning of September, the leaves are already turning brown. Autumn arrives early in Finland and the temperature is quite similar to autumn in England. When I first visited Finland in the autumn, the beautiful colour of the trees in the vast forests astounded me. Of course the best view was had from the aeroplane in which I sat. It wasn't until I experienced this sight that I realised that Finland wasn't full of just pine trees, but in fact had many birch trees as well which added to the wonderful colours. The autumn equinox takes place on 23 September, and from then on, the days get significantly shorter, week by week.

With the longer, darker nights, come darker and drab days. The first snow that appears in October is a welcome sight. Everyone rejoices. The whiteness and brightness of the snow adds lucidity to the days, and winter can truly be said to have arrived. It snows until the end of March with every fresh fall layering upon the previous one until the snow is immeasurably deep. In Lapland, the snow may arrive in September and stay until late June. In Helsinki, in the south, some of the snow will melt away before another fresh layer falls. The winters are cold and the temperature can rise or fall dramatically.

I was in Rovaniemi just before Christmas and was fortunate to experience quite a warm spell. It was around –7°C. However, on the day I was leaving, the temperature had fallen to –32°C overnight. Although, by any measurement, the temperature is cold, the climate is very dry, and provided you are wrapped up warmly the cold doesn't penetrate into your bones like the cold and damp in England. The cold is so dry that you continually have to apply cream to your hands, lips and face. This dryness is the cause of a great amount of static electricity. Your hair will stand on end, even with a good dose of hair conditioner, and you will forever receive little electric shocks. After experiencing a few winter weeks, I begin to dread pressing the button for the lift or reaching for a door handle!

But winter is a magical time in Finland. The snow is absolutely beautiful. When the temperature falls to –10°C, each flake of snow freezes as an individual entity. The light from the street lamps, shining down, makes it look as if you are walking through a field full of sparkling diamonds. Each snowflake twinkles in its own way, with its own colour, and as you walk you can hear the crisp sound of crunching underfoot. For anyone who hasn't experienced this, it is as though you are walking on glass crystals and crushing them underfoot. I will never lose the excitement I feel when I fly into Finland and see the first winter snows. When the landing lights from the aeroplane catch the snowflakes, I automatically think, "Here are my acres of diamonds!"

In the far north of Finland, from 22 November to 20 January, the half-light of morning seeps immediately into the twilight of the evening. This is known as the polar night. In Rovaniemi on the Arctic Circle, there will be about two hours of daylight. By about half past one, whatever daylight there has been, slips into a twilight called blue time. In December, in southern Finland, daylight comes about half past nine and begins to retreat at three. However, by the end of January, the days are noticeably drawing out.

The coldest temperature, –50°C, was measured in Salla, Lapland, in 1985; the highest, 36°C, was recorded in Turku, in 1914.

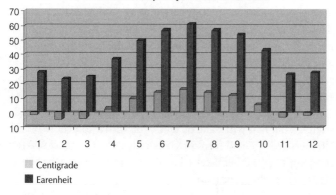

Mean monthly temperatures in Helsinki

Centigrade
Earenheit

POPULATION

The population of Finland is currently just over five million people, giving a density of 17 per sq km. Over half the population live in the three southwestern provinces around Helsinki, Turku and Tampere. Twenty percent of the population, that is one million people, live in the greater Helsinki area.

As with most European nations, the population is ageing. Only about 19% of the population is under fifteen years of age and the middle-aged groups predominate. Nowadays, the average household size is 2.2 people although, around the time of World War II, it would not be uncommon to find families with ten children in them. Fifty-four percent of households live in single-family houses and 43% in apartment blocks, with 77% of the nation being urban dwellers.

The Finns' genetic make-up is 75% the same as the Swedes'. However, the Finnish people are not a homogeneous race. They are the descendants of no less than five different ethnic groups: the Häme people, the Karelians, Savo people, Ostrobothnians and the Sami (Lapps). These people came to Finland by different routes after the last Ice Age. They journeyed from the east, south and west, over a process lasting for several thousand years. These Finno-Ugrians were people of the nomadic tribe who inhabited much of northern Russia. A substantial Indo-European influence over the years has affected the population of Finland, also. As Finland was under the Swedes for over seven hundred years, many Finns, especially in the southwestern part of Finland, now look very Swedish.

There are around 300,000 Swedish-speaking Finns living in Finland along with 4,000 Sami people (Lapps) who live in Finnish Lapland. Around 6% of the nation are of Swedish stock. Finland has the lowest percentage of any European country of resident foreigners. These amount to 2% of the population. There are about 5,000 gypsies who live in the southern half of Finland and, of all the refugees that live there, the majority are Vietnamese or Kurdish.

Chapter Two

FIRST IMPRESSIONS

TRANQUILLITY AND CONFORMITY

Your first impressions of Finland will probably be gleaned from arriving as a passenger at Helsinki airport. This sea of tranquillity really is a foretaste of what greets the visitor in his or her travels around Finland. Helsinki airport really does have to be experienced to be believed. There is none of the hustle and bustle that greets you at most airports, nobody running around shouting and screaming at the top of their voices. If you arrive stressed out from travelling, Helsinki airport is a good place to 'chill out'. You will soon become calm and tranquil.

On my travels, I met up with two Armenian pilots who were on their fourth visit to Finland for flight simulation training. When I asked them what was the one thing that they liked best about Finland their answers were, "Calmness" and "Everyone is so civilised."

In fact, this peace and tranquillity transcends the whole country. You may well ask what is behind this tranquillity. Well, it has been said that the Finns must be the world's most obedient people. There seems to be a plethora of enforced rules and regulations that govern Finnish life. However, as a visitor, you are not aware of the rules and regulations, you just realise that everybody conforms. This conformity can be seen in the décor in homes, the way people dress, the month they take their holidays, the newspapers and magazines they read, and, as I read, who they will vote for in the next election. The Finns themselves joke that of all the EU rules, they obey a hundred and twenty percent of them! Everyone, therefore, has an expectation of how everyone else is going to behave—and they usually do. Being loud is definitely frowned upon.

MOBILE PHONES

The next thing that strikes the visitor is that everybody seems to be using a mobile phone. You wouldn't believe that the Finns are supposed to be the most silent, non-talkative people in the world. Put a phone in their hands, and they will talk away for hours! Even the Finns find this reversal of their national characteristic quite humorous and joke, "How do you get a Finn to talk? Put a phone in his hand!" A recent national advertising campaign in Finland, for mobile phones, conveyed the message, "Helping Finns talk more."

In 1991, Finland inaugurated the first Global System Mobile (GSM) network in the world, and by May 1999, 60% of the population were mobile phone users. The Finns are the highest per capita users of mobile phones in the world. Interestingly, Finland, as a nation, adopted the ordinary telephone earlier than any other country. The Finns go for modern technology in a big way, and constantly look for ways of using it in their everyday lives. A mobile phone can be used to operate vending machines; the cost of the chocolate bar is added to the user's telephone bill. Even the smallest companies have all the latest technological gadgets.

I remember watching three gentlemen, in the quiet of a hotel breakfast-room, sitting at the same table having breakfast. None of them were taking much notice of the others for they were all too busy talking on their phones. It is extremely common to see people in a restaurant get up from the table, whilst answering their phone, and walk to a secluded spot to carry on their conversation. In Finnish society, it is considered good manners to excuse yourself from the company of others to conduct your conversation in private. So important is the mobile phone to a Finn that I concluded, shortly after I arrived in Finland, that the term 'coffee break' was a misnomer and renamed it 'telephone time'.

The pervasiveness of the phone culture was brought home to my family in an amusing incident in Lapland. We had decided to spend a few days before Christmas, experiencing the snow and the wilderness and went on a reindeer safari. It was the first time any of us had ever been to this part of the world. Accompanied by only two reindeers, a dog and our guide, we set out across a frozen lake on our journey into nowhere. After half an hour, civilisation seemed thousands of miles away from us. Romantic notions of trekking in the wilderness were soon obliterated by a ringing in the jacket pocket of our guide—it was his mobile phone!

On a reindeer safari

The Finns are, also, the highest Internet users in the world, along with the Scandinavian countries, Iceland and the USA. In fact Joensuu, which is also one of the most eastern towns in Europe, has now laid cables into twenty thousand of the twenty-two thousand homes in the town.

CLEANLINESS

The next thing a visitor to Finland will notice is its cleanliness. At Helsinki airport the floors positively shine, and the toilets and all facilities are immaculately clean. The Finns take a great pride in their environment, and you will never see rubbish and litter lying around. It just isn't in the Finns' nature to dirty their environment, and you will soon be frowned upon if you throw rubbish in public places. Hotel rooms, restaurants, shops and even public transport will all appear clean and tidy to the foreign visitor. The focus on cleanliness is all part of the Finnish national pride.

One of the great things in Finland is that public conveniences are well-equipped. There is always one large toilet cubicle which has a hand-held shower, washbasin, mirror and more than adequate space to manoeuvre in. In addition, parent and baby rooms will have complimentary nappies, a baby-changing mat and a potty.

CUSTOMER CARE

Something will strike the visitor to Finland as peculiarly odd—the Finns' attitude to customer care. They haven't got any, or so it seems. This may sound very harsh but, in truth, the Finns address customer care in a completely different way from the approach British, Asians or Americans would be used to. Herein lies the first real culture shock that most visitors to Finland will experience.

One evening, I was sitting with a colleague of mine in a hotel restaurant. I had ordered my evening meal from the menu, and she had decided that she wanted just a plain ham sandwich. She went into some detail to explain to the waitress that all she required was two slices of bread, plain, with plain ham in the middle. She stipulated that she wanted "no green stuff, no red stuff, no fruity bits either," just a plain ham sandwich. My dinner arrived, her sandwich didn't. I had almost finished my meal when her sandwich eventually arrived. In all its glory, with all the greenery, the red bits and the fruity bits, came her 'plain' ham sandwich. When my colleague quizzed the waitress, she was told this was how the sandwich was served, and if she didn't want all the other bits and pieces, my colleague could take them out; they wouldn't mind.

It's also very difficult to get served in a Finnish restaurant, once your initial order is received. You can never seem to catch the waitress's eye, so you might well have to resort to gesticulating madly. This usually provokes a quick, but dismissive nod, as the waitress walks off in the opposite direction. This leaves you wondering whether she will return. It is rare that anyone will come over to ask whether you would like another drink. I recall a time I called a waitress over to complain that my soup was not hot. She commiserated with me, said, "Shame." and ran away quickly. There have been occasions when I have stood up to leave a restaurant in order to get my bill, so that I could pay.

These incidents might lead the reader to think that the Finns really don't care about the customer, but nothing could be further from the truth. You have to understand the Finns' psyche in order to understand that they really do care. The first incident with the ham sandwich demonstrates the Finns' desire to genuinely give you what they think you really ought to have—not what you ordered. I experienced this on another occasion when I tried to buy a pair of boots. The assistant kept bringing me different models to try on rather than the ones I originally asked for. In the second case, the Finns believe that it is an invasion of your privacy to have eye contact, so they leave you alone in silence and without any contact to enjoy your meal, and it's up to you to get hold of them. The Finns don't normally complain and they find it very difficult to handle a complaint. Therefore, when I complained about the soup, the waitress really didn't know what to do about it. I have since found that if I have cold soup, I have to say, "Excuse me my soup is only warm. Would you please take it away and make it hot." This allows them to understand what I want. The Finns are not used to pushing themselves forward, and in a very egalitarian society, they are not used to being subservient. It is therefore, up to you as the customer, to make your wishes clear. In a restaurant, apart from asking about dessert, they will not come and ask you if you want anything else. In other words, you will not be 'sold to'. This will be seen as being an invasion of your privacy and an interruption of your personal silence.

REVERSE LOGIC

On the occasion when I was trying to buy boots, it became obvious that my feet were too wide for the narrow fitting Finnish shoes. The assistant told me that lots of people have the same problem and she wondered why there had not yet been devised an operation to cure wide feet. Never did it occur to her that they could make the shoes wider rather than have customers suffer the painful machinations of a surgical operation. Often I find the Finns coming at a situation from the opposite direction from me. Some foreigners regard this attitude as a form of arrogance but I prefer to think of it as reverse logic—I do find it funny at times.

The Finns do not like to disappoint you or let you down and, as a result, they rarely make 'draft' timetables or 'pencilled in' appointments. They will let you know when they are confident that a meeting can be made, and you are expected to jump to it. This is the one trait that most annoys people who have diaries full of 'pencilled in' appointments!

TRAFFIC

The next thing that strikes a visitor, especially from the more crowded parts of Europe, is the lack of traffic in Finland. I even think that the word 'traffic' is a misnomer when applied to the vehicles on Finnish roads. At certain hours of the day in Finnish towns you really have to play a game of spot-the-car because, normally, the roads are very quiet. Generally, Finnish families only have one car and children make their own way to school; so there are no school runs and rush hours as in Britain, for example. Junctions will normally clear in one turn of the traffic lights.

There was a bus strike in the town of Tampere just recently, and my Finnish colleague, Timo, experienced a few queues building up at each junction for the first time ever and was quite baffled as to the reason why. When he met me the next time, he told me that he had actually seen a 'traffic jam' in Finland and realised it had been caused by the bus strike. My French colleague Christine, who lives in Marseilles, said when she first came to Finland she was absolutely "stunned at seeing all these empty roads."

DAYLIGHT HOURS

The next thing that makes a big impact on visitors coming to Finland in the summer months, is the length of the days. The memories I have of my first trip to Finland, in the summer of 1997, when the weather was gloriously hot, are of me sitting at 7:30 a.m., in the market square, under the shade of an umbrella, drinking coffee and watching people on their way to work. The sun, already high in the sky, penetrated through the umbrella to warm my skin. It was quite warm even though it was still early in the day. In contrast, I have sat out late at night reading a book by the natural light in the sky. At 11:30 p.m. it is only just beginning to become dusk. The Finns, of course, are quite used to light nights but I can never resist going for a walk, at midnight, by the shores of a lake, along the banks of a river, or in the town square.

My greatest memory, and the one that will stay with me all my life, is of the moment I stepped off the plane at Kuopio. It was half past midnight, and the sun was just beginning to set. The sky was a beautiful colour of puce pink with purple clouds. It was just an absolutely unbelievable sight and birds were still flocking to make their way to their nests. Half an hour later the sun was up and it was definitely dawn.

One thing that astounds me (and all the foreign colleagues I know) is that the Finns often close the blinds as soon as the sun shines, winter or summer. They cannot have a room too bright!

IMPRESSIONS OF A RETURNED FINN

I recall one occasion when I was travelling by train from Helsinki to Joensuu. I met a lady Lutheran priest. She had recently returned to Finland with her family having spent two years in Tenerife. We talked for a long while and she described to me how she was seeing the Finns through Spanish eyes, realising how much she and her family had changed their behaviour in the time they had been away. She said the things she most noticed were:

- an increase in the use of mobile phones.
- everyone is drinking beer.
- at first they were very noisy in restaurants, until they noticed that no one else was.
- as a family they have had to learn to be quiet again.
- the Finns don't smile.
- they seem not to be happy unlike the Spanish.
- the Finns are impatient and have to get things done quickly.
- the Finns are impatient in restaurants. They don't want to wait for *good* food to be cooked. They expect their meal quickly.
- the stillness, the silence, and the calm.

– Chapter Three –

HISTORY, POLITICS AND THE ECONOMY

Many people are surprised to learn that the country we know as Finland today is a very young country—it was declared an independent republic only on 6 December 1917. For almost seven centuries the Finns were under Swedish rule and then, for over a century, under Russian rule. Perhaps this is the reason why the Finns are so enormously proud of their country and nationhood, seemingly more patriotic than many other nationals. Also, it could be why many foreigners know nothing much about the country although they have all heard of it.

ORIGINS

Much of Finnish history before the twelfth century has been passed on through folklore with very few written records concerning the Finns and their country. In A.D.98, Tacitus mentions a people called the Fenni in the Germania, which is how the population of present-day southwest Finland came to be known. The inhabitants of the interior

35

were called Häme people; a name derived from an old Baltic word meaning 'an inhabitant of the interior.'

The first settlers came to Finland about 7,000 B.C. They occupied the coastal lowlands of southern Finland. They lived by hunting elk and by fishing in the Baltic Sea, which was then a freshwater lake. The land was no more than a bleak, tundra-like terrain without its present-day characteristics. Around 6,000 years ago, the Sami arrived from the East. There are many competing theories as to the origins of the Finns, but it seems that the southwestern part of Finland was settled by boat people from western Europe and the eastern part by nomadic tribes from Russia. These people came from the surrounding areas of the Ural Mountains and the River Volga and settled to become the Finns, Estonians and Karelians of today. From them developed the Finno-Ugrian language. These peoples displaced the Sami who migrated further north to Lapland and are today's Lapps (Sami in Finnish).

Two distinct cultures evolved which were influenced by both the east and the west. The two Finnish tribes, the Hamenites in the west and the Karelians in the east, constantly warred with each other. Trading links were set up with the Estonians and the Swedish Vikings. After about A.D. 800, the Vikings began spreading eastwards through the Åland Islands, Finland and into Russia, ruling Novgorod and eventually reaching Kiev in A.D. 862. The Karelians traded with Novgorod, supplying them with furs and skins. This contact influenced the Karelian culture enormously. Their craftsmen adopted Byzantine motifs for use in art and jewellery designs and these can still be seen today as 'traditional Finnish' designs. The Karelians acquired their Orthodox form of Christianity through contact with the East and Russian monks later travelled north to convert the Lapps . In the meantime, missionaries from Sweden began to convert the tribes in the west of Finland. An English missionary, Bishop Henry of Uppsala, later became the patron saint of Finland.

BEING RULED

In the eleventh and twelfth centuries, Finland became a buffer between many rival powers. Sweden had established a strong monarchy. Novgorod had become a powerful military base. The expanding Danish kingdom was successfully resisting Swedish supremacy and founded the city of Tallin, in Estonia, in 1219. To the east, the Teutonic knights were encroaching on the lands south of the Gulf of Finland and were busy warring with the Danes as they tried to take hold of the lands along the Baltic coast. The Finns had not joined together as one nation state of their own and were subjected to influences from all these sources. In fact, they were divided into three main groups: the Suomalaiset (as the Finns call themselves today), the Hamalaiset (the Hamenites) and the Karjalaiset (the Karelians).

In the middle of the twelfth century, the Swedish throne was occupied by King Erik. The Pope had issued instructions that the position of the Church in Scandinavia needed to be strengthened. As a Catholic, Erik led a crusade to convert the Finns to Christianity. He was accompanied by Bishop Henry who was later left in Finland to consolidate the gains of Erik's crusade while Erik returned to Sweden. Although not the first, it was this crusade that established the beginnings of an organised Finnish Church. A cathedral was built in Turku in 1229 and dedicated to St. Erik and St. Henry. The bones of St. Henry were laid to rest there in 1290. In spite of the fact that the Finnish Church was under the supervision of a Danish See, it was the Swedes who ultimately dominated south and west Finland. Eastern Finland was still heavily influenced by the Byzantine Empire, through Kiev and Novgorod. Turku, in southwest Finland, became the centre of both religious and civil authority in Finland. Swedish occupation began in earnest in 1249. A number of incentives were devised to attract Swedish settlers to Finland. Large estates were created. Tax concessions were given. Soon the upper layer of Finnish society comprised Catholic bishops and Swedish nobility. Many privileges were granted to Swedish soldiers of the Royal Army to entice them to settle. The Swedish settlers began to colonise the coastal regions of southwest Finland and along the Gulf of Finland. They brought with them their language which established Swedish as a major language in Finland.

The next hundred years saw conflict and skirmishes between the Swedes and the rulers of Novgorod as each tried to snatch land away from the other. Eventually, in 1323, a peace treaty was signed which established the border between the two countries as running in a northwesterly direction from a location near today's St. Petersburg, in Russia, to Oulu, in northwest Finland. This brought about a period of relative calm and, as a result, Swedish influence gained strength in the southwestern half of Finland. This influence brought about contact with Western Europe and Roman Catholicism. Over the next three centuries, Finland became firmly part of the Swedish kingdom adopting its laws and administrative practices. There was little friction between the Swedes and the Finns. The Swedes settled along the coastal lands whilst the Finns lived, for the most part, in the interior. They shared religious, judicial and administrative practices and co-existed peacefully. In the meantime, the northeastern half of Finland was dominated by cultural links with the east and the Eastern Orthodox Church.

In 1527, King Gustav Vasa of Sweden adopted the Lutheran faith and this set Sweden and Finland firmly on the road to establishing Lutheranism as the official religion. Wanting to expand his territories, he enticed his Finnish subjects to push forward the boundaries set down in the treaty with Russia and encroach upon the Savo and Kainuu areas. Turku became firmly established as the capital of Finland from where the governor general presided from his castle.

During the 'Golden Age' of Sweden, in the seventeenth century, Finland was considered an integral part of Sweden, and the Finns were considered loyal subjects of the Swedish monarch. The official language was Swedish, Stockholm was the de facto capital, and by

Swedish decree Finland began to grow and prosper. Schools and churches were established, ironworks built, transport systems created and a chain of castle defences built to protect against Russian attack. Trade increased but the burgher class was predominantly Swedish as few Finns made a living from business. The ethnic Finns were largely peasant farmers, forced into a type of feudal serfdom, who had to lease land from their Swedish overlords.

The 1700s saw Finland fought over and occupied on numerous occasions. The Russians, under Peter the Great, seized much of Finland and even conquered the west coast. In trying to regain its lost territories, Sweden warred with Russia for the best part of one hundred years. In doing so, it won back land which had to be later ceded to Russia, which they then won and lost again. Then the Napoleonic Wars were to have a lasting impact on Finland. After Tsar Alexandra I and Napoleon signed the Treaty of Tilsit, Russia attacked Finland in 1808. Sweden ceded Finland to Russia in 1809 and the Swedish king, Gustav IV Adolf, lost his crown to Napoleon.

Helsinki Cathedral

Finland became an autonomous grand duchy with its own senate with only major decisions having to be approved by the Tsar. Russia encouraged Finland to develop as a country, made education available to all, established universities and transferred the capital to Helsinki in 1812. Finland began to benefit greatly from this annexation. In the mid-1800s Finland issued its own postage stamps and gained its own currency, the markka. However, the Finnish independence movement was gathering momentum. One of the first to encourage independence was a teacher, Adolf Ivor Arvidsson, who stated: "Swedes we are not, Russians we will not be, so let us be Finns."

Around this time Elias Lönnrot, one of the central figures in Finnish literature, published his work the *Kalevala* which was an epic poem based on the spoken folklore of the many Finnish 'tribes' around the country. This became a catalyst for the swell of the independence movement because it came at a time when the Finns were beginning to think about who they were as a nation. For the first time ever, their own history and culture were written down and all could learn what it really meant to be Finnish.

The 1860s are referred to as 'The Hunger Years' when it has been said that almost one third of the population died from starvation. Many rural advisory centres were established to help farmers manage their farms more efficiently and effectively so they could increase food production. Farmers associations started and the 'seeds of knowledge' were passed on in schools.

TWENTIETH CENTURY HISTORY

In 1906, a new single-house parliament, the Eduskunta, was created. Men and women alike from all stations in life were given full voting rights. Finland was the first European country to grant women full political rights—universal and equal suffrage. In spite of the many advances that Finland had enjoyed under the Russians, the Finns still felt oppressed. They had had a hundred years of ruling themselves as an autonomous grand duchy. Then Tsar Nicholas I attempted to turn

Finland into a mere Russian province causing an outcry. Finnish intellectuals and artists were stirred by this greater oppression and helped create a surge of nationalism. Jean Sibelius, Finland's famous composer, composed his masterpiece *Finlandia* and Akseli Gallén-Kallela, a painter and architect, painted scenes from the *Kalevala*. This provided a core around which a new nation could rally. The Finns became emotionally ripe for independence. The Russian Revolution of 1917 resulted in the seizing of power by the communists and the ousting of the tsar. As a result, the Finnish senate declared independence on 6 December 1917 and Finland was recognised as an independent state by the Russians themselves just one month later.

INDEPENDENCE

One of the perplexing questions for the new nation was whether it should become a republic or a monarchy. The Reds, a revolutionary unit comprising the working-classes, aspired to a Russian-style socialist independent nation. The Whites, comprising the newly established government, favoured becoming a monarchy based on the German model. Vladimir Lenin, however, recognising he would need support in the on-going World War I, decided to give the Finnish Reds 10,000 guns and lend them troops to attack the Whites (Finland's official military force) in Vyborg. This gave rise to the Civil War.

The poor harvest of 1917 meant the Finns were once again facing starvation. The widespread devastation of Russia meant that no food supplies would come from there. Aid committees were set up in Sweden, Britain and USA to send food for distribution by the government but the dilemma arose to whom it should be sent. The White Government appeared to be in alliance with the Germans, then the enemy of Europe, and the Reds were supported by Russia who had just exacted a bloody revolution.

On 28 January 1918 the Civil War started in earnest. It was fought on two fronts. The Reds strove for revolution in Helsinki whilst the

Whites, led by General Carl Gustaf Mannerheim and supported by the Germans, fought Russian forces near Vaasa. The new nation was divided. The Reds claimed the South whilst the Whites stood their ground in the North. The Civil War lasted 108 days and claimed the lives of 30,000 Finns. The Whites eventually became the victors under the military prowess of General Mannerheim.

The Whites extracted a bloody vengeance on their defeated enemies. Reds and their families were captured and locked up in prison camps where thousands died through starvation and neglect. An estimated 10,000 people died in these camps. By 1924 the problem of political prisoners was gone though bitterness lingered on through another generation.

The Civil War ended on 16 May 1918. The Prince of Hessen, Friedrich Karl, was asked to become king of Finland by the Eduskunta on 9 October 1918. However, just one month later, Germany was defeated in World War I. The Prince of Hessen declined the offer and the political model Finland wanted to adopt became discredited. Finland then chose a Republican State model and Professor K.J. Ståhlberg, a liberal-minded constitutional lawyer, became its first president (1919-1925).

The Constitution of 1919, whose main architect was Ståhlberg, retained the single-house parliament that was established in 1906. It also stated that Finnish and Swedish would be the national languages of the new republic and established the right of citizens to use their mother tongue before the law courts and administrative authorities. Records and documents were to be written in the mother tongue and this would be guaranteed by law. Regions would be unilingual unless a minority group existed which represented over 10% of the local population. This would be reviewed statistically every 10 years. Helsinki and Turku were to be bilingual. At the time, Swede-Finns accounted for only 11% of the total population. The government recognised that tolerance and accommodation of this minority would best serve the interest of the country as a whole.

The 1930s saw the fledgling nation at a low ebb. Civil War skirmishes continued with right and left-wing extremists battering and bruising political life. Attempts were made to outlaw Marxism which resulted in fascism being made illegal. Fighting broke out between university students of the two language groups and a bitter language war ensued which shook the administration, universities and cultural circles. Finland developed close ties with Germany partly in response to the threat of their predatory giant Russian neighbour.

Before World War I the Finns were said to be the most sober people in Europe. The consumption of liquor in Finland was decreasing year by year. In June 1919 the Government introduced prohibition which was generally recognised as a sound strategic policy by the vast majority of the nation. By 1931, the law was repealed. It had turned out to be an economic disaster, creating a lucrative black economy. The State Alcohol Corporation was established, with the right to sell liquor. Thus the importation and distribution of alcohol became state-owned and state-directed.

During the time between the two world wars, this new struggling nation gained an international reputation for bravery, honesty, integrity and hard work. In spite of the fact that the economy was still agrarian-based and two thirds of the population worked on farms, Finland became the only country to pay its debts to the USA. Towards the end of the 1920s, the country's industrial production was increasing and there was an export boom in forest-related products which provided much needed foreign currency. At the same time, Finland began to shine in athletics with its sporting hero, Paavo Nurmi (the Flying Finn) winning seven gold medals in long-distance running in three Olympics. Continuing success in athletics led to Helsinki being chosen as the venue for the 1940 Olympic Games, which were eventually held in 1952 due to the interruption of World War II.

With war clouds gathering over Europe, the Soviet and German foreign ministers signed a pact of non-aggression on 23 August 1939. The pact laid the way for Germany to have a free hand in Lithuania whilst the Soviet Union could move against Finland, Estonia and Latvia; Poland would be divided between the two powers. The Finns hoped to escape the conflict by declaring their neutrality. However, 1939 saw the outbreak of war in Europe into which Finland was reluctantly dragged on 30 November when the Red Army invaded, arguing that its security needed southeastern Karelia and some other military areas by the sea.

The 'Winter War' as it became known was especially tragic as temperatures during an extremely harsh winter fell to –40°C and soldiers, on both sides, died in their thousands. After 100 days the Finns were defeated, the southeastern part of Karelia was ceded to the Russians and half a million refugees flooded into Finland. The Soviet Union stepped up efforts to wrest more land from the Finns and in desperation Finland turned to Germany for help. Although there was never any formal agreement between the two countries, German troops were allowed right of passage through Finland to Sweden. When hostilities between Germany and Russia broke out in June 1941, the 'Continuation War' between Finland and the Soviet Union began. The valiant struggle of the small Finnish army resulted in them repossessing Karelia and even land they had lost in the eighteenth century. In the summer of 1944, the Russians overwhelmed the Finns. Mannerheim, then aged over 70, negotiated an armistice with the Soviets and then began to oust German troops from Lapland. This struggle lasted until the general surrender in the spring of 1945.

The nation's struggle for independence and the heroic and successful fight to retain that independence during World War II against immense odds came with a price. Finland was forced to cede territory to the Soviet Union and pay it heavy war reparations.

POST-WAR FINLAND

Dreams of a 'Greater Finland', which had been the aspiration of a whole generation, were discarded as the nation faced up to the massive burden of trying to repay its debts. Finland's reparations to the Soviet Union were mostly paid in heavy engineering. Once again there was a shortage of food, everything was rationed and poverty was widespread. In 1948 the Treaty of Friendship, Cooperation and Mutual Assistance was signed which bound the two countries in a semi-military agreement. Finland still laid claim to its neutrality but the shadow of its giant neighbour meant that Finland had to bow to the wishes of the Soviet Union, even in terms of its own domestic politics.

The Finnish president from 1956 to 1981, Urho Kekkonen, was a master diplomat who became one of the great leaders of his time. He managed to grasp the nettle in the difficult relationship with the Soviet Union. He gained fame abroad as host of the initial meeting of the 'Conference on Security and Cooperation in Europe', held in Helsinki in 1975. He led Finland as a founding member of the Nordic Council. As a result, it enjoyed the same benefits as Scandinavia: free movement of labour, a passport-free zone, joint research and educational programmes and pursuit of the same type of welfare programme.

The Soviet Union still exercised a great deal of influence over Finland up until the late 1980s, blocking its membership of the European Community and minimalising any influence from the United States. By choosing a path of neutrality Finland opted out of the Arms Race.

During the 1960s many people migrated to the South and large urban areas grew around Helsinki. Many areas in the North and East lost a large percentage of their young people. Self-sufficiency in food was reached by 1960 with bigger farms and more productive techniques to increase the food supply. This in itself created new problems: what to do with overproduction and how to employ everyone. The food industry became focused on quality and environmental aspects:

- animal husbandry
- dairy farming
- organic farming
- crop cultivation
- berry production

- fishery centres
- regional centres for country women and homemakers

During this time, Finland's advance in industry, farming, trade, commerce and the professions was driven by sheer profit. However, from the outset, this drive was not aimed at the gain of the individual citizen but at the welfare of the nation as a whole. Through the twentieth century, increasing attention has been paid to finding solutions to social and economic problems through legislation and public expenditure.

TODAY

Finland suffered more than most European nations during the recession of the early 1990s. The Soviet Union broke up leaving debts unpaid, the markka was devalued, many companies closed, unemployment rose from 3% to 20%, and the tax burden increased alarmingly. In 1995, Finland elected to join the European Union and the economy took a turn for the better: food instantly became cheaper and the country received considerable financial aid through EU assistance with regional development grants. However, the traditional market place for Finnish goods, the Soviet Union, has not been restored and Finland has had to find new markets.

The break-up of the Soviet Union into several smaller states has considerably changed the balance of power within the Baltic region. Finland still vigorously pursues its policy of strict neutrality. It has retained commercial ties with the new republics and has offered its technological know-how in environmental matters and financial assistance to buy food supplies.

As Fred Singleton wrote in his book *A Short History of Finland*, "Finland's greatest contribution to the twentieth century lies simply in the fact that it has survived intact as a nation state, dedicated to the principles of parliamentary democracy, and that it has been able to maintain a welfare state, rising living standards, despite the battering it has taken from a hostile world during the brief period of its national independence. A small weak nation learned to live alongside a predatory giant neighbour—without losing its sense of national identity."

Finland has become a champion of civil liberties. In their surveys on the degree of freedom experienced by citizens in various countries, Amnesty International always has Finland appearing near the top list. In a 1998 survey by the United Nations, Finland was rated fifth in the world in terms of quality of life. This survey measured education, income, health and life expectancy. In 1999, Finnish children were deemed to be the healthiest in Europe along with the Swedes. Indeed, this small nation has come a long way since independence.

THE ECONOMY

The loss of Viipuri (now Vyborg) and the manufacturing centres of Karelia during World War II deprived Finland of a substantial amount of its resources. One third of its hydro electricity, 25% of its chemical pulp production, 12% of its productive forests and 9% of its arable land were ceded to the Soviet Union. By the end of World War II, the Finnish economy had virtually collapsed. The reparation schedule imposed on Finland by the Soviets was to be paid in metal goods, heavy engineering products, ships and electrical cables. An intensive programme of investment, mostly state-financed, was undertaken to bring Finland up to the level where it could begin to make reparation. Unlike some other countries devastated by the war, Finland received no foreign aid to help rebuild its broken economy.

The transformation from a rural society to an urban industrialised country had to be quick. Driven by the need to make war reparations to the Soviet Union, industrialisation made great strides. The reparation schedule eventually ended in 1952. For the next two decades after this, Finland began to prosper. The country recognised that it could not compete in the world of mass production along with countries like the USA and Britain. However, it has become among the top ten industrialised nations of the world, specialising in products in which skill, design, originality and flair account for more than bulk, volume and mass production. It sells its expertise all over the world. Amongst other projects, the Finns designed and built the roads in Tanzania, and Finnish scientists help keep Finland at the cutting edge of new technologies in the fields of electronics and timber products. Production is concentrated on high-value technology-orientated products, computer-controlled mechanical systems, special types of vehicles, mobile phones and shipping.

Timber is still the raw material of greatest economic value and it is fascinating to see the enormously long trucks, loaded with freshly felled logs, driving across the country. Finland is the most heavily wooded country in Europe. Sixty-three percent of the forests are in the hands of private owners, which equates to one in five families. Sixty-six percent of the total output of the forestry industry is exported. Timber, furniture, paper, pulp, cellulose and various chemicals are its products and Finnish scientists lead the way in finding innovative new ways to use wood and its derivatives. Finland has the largest copper mines in Europe, exports zinc and nickel, but has to import all its oil and coal.

Finland went through one of the worst recessions experienced by any western economy in the 1990s. Twenty-five percent of Finnish exports were to the Soviet Union and its demise cost Finland dearly. Where it was once the most expensive country in the world (1990), Finland soon became one of the cheapest. From almost full employment, 500,000 jobs disappeared within two years. Finland suffered 20% unemployment, the second highest in Europe. This proved to be an unimaginable burden on the state and in an effort to reduce the deficit, the government imposed heavy spending cuts. However, spending on education and grants for private research and development were increased. By 1995 Finland had become a net exporter of know-how and high-tech products. Exports now account for about 40% of GDP, with IT contributing the largest share.

In 1900, 85% of all exports were forestry-related. Now these account for only one-third of all exports. Finland is the second largest exporter of paper in the world. Nokia is the world's largest manufacturer of mobile phones. Metal mining, technology and engineering together make up exports almost as sizeable as paper. The service and construction industries play an increasingly important part in the Finnish economy.

Economic structure of Finland : Employed persons by industry,
Fourth quarter 1999 (Source: Statistics Finland)

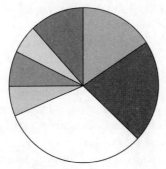

■ Commerce 16%
■ Industry 21%
　 Misc. Services 32%
　 Construction 6%
■ Transport/Communications 7%
　 Agriculture/Forestry 6%
■ Financial Service 12%

Since the early 1990s, Finland has made a remarkable economic recovery. By the end of 1999, industrial production had grown by record-breaking figures. The biggest increase took place in the electronics and electrotechnical industry, where the growth rate accelerated to 40%. The primary factor boosting growth in industrial production is exports. Unemployment is down to 9.5% and inflation, which has consistently hovered between 1% and 2% annually, has recently risen to 3.7% (December 1999). The trade unions, who are a powerful force in the Finnish economy with 83% of the work force, allowed salaries to be pegged at 1.7% over two years, thus helping to keep inflation down. There are strict rules governing working hours and holidays, as Finland pursues a very generous social welfare programme. Finland was one of 11 countries whose economy qualified to begin using the new Euro currency at the beginning of 1999. (Their strict alcohol laws have been relaxed since joining the EU.) There are very close links between Finland and Estonia and the opening up of the Baltic States with a population of 40 million could prove to offer Finland a great competitive advantage.

Ten years ago, Finland was a closed society. Foreigners were unable to work in the country unless they had a very specialised job, and those who married a Finn found that the formalities took forever to grant them the right to live and work there. Finland was like a fortress. Foreigners were not allowed to own land or property without a special dispensation at ministerial level and they were not allowed to hold the majority of shares in any business.

Figures released at the end of 1999 showed that 67% of the Finnish population had mobile phone subscriptions and Finland is about to have a third GSM operator. One of the most interesting applications of the mobile phone is seen in health care, in which the need to improve service efficiency grows as the population ages. Innovations by small technology companies have brought Finland to the forefront of development in this field. One service creates better conditions for diabetes patients to care for themselves by allowing them, via mobile phone and the Internet, to give information on blood glucose measurements, dosage of insulin used, meals and exercise to a database, thus eliminating the need for patients in sparsely populated areas to travel long distances to see a specialist.

At the outset of the year 2000, Finland is in a strong position to become one of the world's most successful economies.

GOVERNMENT AND POLITICS

In 1906 the 'Diet of Four Estates' became a single chamber parliament of 200 seats called the Eduskunta. The new parliament was elected by equal and universal suffrage in a secret vote, which included women. The Finnish Constitution came into effect in 1919. The voting age at present is 18.

The Finns are governed by means of a presidential republic. The executive government comprises the president, in council with the prime minister and the cabinet. The president is elected for a six-year term. Finland currently has a woman president, the Speaker of Parliament is a woman and now for the first time ever the opposition is also led by a woman (See *Families and Women's Role*). The prime minister is elected every four years by the 200-member Eduskunta. Eduskunta members serve a four-year term and are elected from fourteen electoral districts. The parliament is a single chamber—unicameral. The Åland Islands are self-governing and have their own parliament (*Landsting*).

Many Finns are floating voters and easily have ten different political parties to choose from. The government often becomes a coalition usually consisting of two or three of the largest parties, with one or more smaller parties. The largest political party is the Social Democratic Party. Other major political parties in Finland include the Agrarian Centre Party, the Conservative National Coalition Party, the Left-wing Alliance, the Greens, the Swedish People's Party and the Christian Union. I found fascinating the fact that at the last election, in March 1999, one politician thought it would be wise to visit southern Spain and canvass for votes there, because there were so many Finns living in that part of the world.

The current government is headed by Paavo Lipponen, 58, who is in his second term of office. The government has been nicknamed 'The Rainbow' because it contains such a broad base from the political spectrum—linking Social Democrats with Christian Democrats and other conservatives of that ilk. Paavo Lipponen has led the Social Democratic Party since 1993 and formed his first rainbow coalition in 1995. The party lost a considerable amount of ground in the 1999 elections, but retained its position as the largest in the parliament. The conservative National Coalition Party won nearly as many seats as the Social Democrats. The most recent election polled 68% of votes which produced the following results: Social Democratic Party 51 seats, Finnish Centre 48, National Coalition 46, Left-wing Alliance 20, Swedish People's Party 12, Greens 11, Christian League 10, True Finns 1, Reform Group 1.

Local government is divided into provinces (*laani*) with each headed by a prefect. The functions of local government include regional planning, transport, health and education. These are administered by rural and municipal communes.

Holding the EU Presidency for the final six months of the twentieth century helped raise the international profile of Finland. During this time, policies concerned with the 'Northern Dimension' were passed. One decision which was taken was to extend the European Investment Bank's coverage to Russia, allowing for the planning of a road bypass of St. Petersburg. A road link between St. Petersburg and the Finnish border is now under construction.

THE MILITARY

Finland has a very small 'professional' standing army but has a large reserve force. Young men of 18 are expected to do their national service. They have a choice of either doing military service, with or without arms, or community service. This can be for a period of six, nine or twelve months (eleven months for officers and non-commissioned officers in reserves). Since 1995, women have been allowed to volunteer for national service. Some people can opt to do national service when they are older. For men, reserve duty continues until at least the age of fifty. Conscientious objectors have the right to choose non-military forms of national service.

Defence spending is low relative to other European countries at 1.5% of GDP and 5.5% of the total government budget. The Finnish army has some Swedish-only units. The most notable role that the Finnish army plays is in peacekeeping activities for the United Nations and they serve all over the world.

The police is part of national government and operates under the control of the Ministry of the Interior. Local police are supervised by provincial authorities and organised into town police departments and rural police districts. These manage routine police work. The mobile police assist local police where necessary, but they are responsible for traffic safety and riot control and operate at a national level. The security police are there to prevent subversion and espionage. The central criminal police maintain centralised criminal files, mount extensive investigations and keep contact with foreign police forces. The coast guards and border police are charged with the security of the border areas and, in times of war, have a military role.

Chapter Four

THE FINNS

The Finns do not consider themselves Scandinavian, nor do they like to admit that any part of them may be Russian. However, Finnish traditions owe something to both cultures. The old traditions bind people together. Yet the Finns are very modern and very technologically driven. They have a strong national identity, a deep-rooted love for their ancestral land, and a national pride that envelopes them, instilled in them from birth and through good education.

It has been said that a characteristic of the Finns is their sameness. They do not like to stand out in a crowd, and their mode of dress is very similar to everyone else's. The Finns, of course, disagree with this over-generalisation and consider themselves very individualistic. However, an example which illustrates this trait is they do not celebrate people's achievements. Whilst births and marriages may be news on the office grapevine, outstanding achievements in professional life, educational examinations or industry awards, seem to be swept under the carpet. Any open broadcast would be seen as bragging, which isn't good. Being humble is regarded as a virtue.

The Finns have had a long struggle for emancipation, and a continuing struggle to survive once independence was won. This fact alone has seemingly strengthened the resolve in each and every Finn. They have an inbuilt resilience to survive prolonged hardship. This Finnish trait is called '*sisu*', or guts. Even if all looks lost, a Finn with *sisu* will fight on valiantly until final defeat, and then he still won't give up. *Sisu* is a quality that is central to their being—a tough independent personality.

The Finns remain a forest people at heart. They are naturally reserved, especially towards foreigners, and are likely to seem very formal and aloof. In a culture where silence is a virtue, extreme chattiness is viewed with surprise or suspicion. In a culture where personal space is a right not a privilege, a handshake is always appropriate, but a hug and kiss is not.

A CLASSLESS SOCIETY

Finland is a society where few have too much and even fewer have too little. One thing that particularly strikes visitors to Finland is the apparent absence of class distinctions in education, in everyday social life and in the protocol of public life. It has been said that without an overseas empire or a native monarchy and aristocracy, there has been no opportunity for racial, social or class superiority to take root.

The relative absence of social barriers in their own society, has led the Finns to be very well liked and accepted in many parts of the globe. The Finns have been very successful missionaries in Africa because they were seen to be of European stock, but without the taint of white supremacy and the colonial attitude. No one resents the Finns when they arrive abroad. There are many foreign aid programmes and development programmes supported by Finland, especially in East Africa. The roads in Tanzania were built with Finnish support. The Finnish are particularly well accepted in their UN peacekeeping roles and many political summits are held in Helsinki, as Finland is seen as a country with 'no axe to grind' and no historical alliances.

One Finnish friend told me, "We have no social class. It is very impolite to admit or think in terms of social classes." Of course, Finnish society is not without snobbery, but it is said to hark back to the days of Swedish nobility and German barons. There exists an elitism in some Swede-Finn minority. Some speak little or no Finnish, by speaking Swedish at home and by attending Swedish- speaking schools and university. Although they have a Finnish passport, they see themselves as superior and refuse to integrate in Finnish society or speak Finnish. Also, they have no wish for their children to be bilingual. The majority of Finns do not witness this, though an English friend of mine who works in Helsinki knows a small 'clique' who keep themselves very separate.

One American lady I met, who had worked for a Finnish company in the USA for over twenty years, spoke about the Finnish 'old guard' as being very arrogant and superior. Nowadays, she explained, the Finns are quite changed and really very hospitable. An Englishman I encountered, who is married to a Finn and has been living in Finland for ten years, told me that when he first came to Finland he was treated as a second-class citizen. "Things changed," he said, "when they joined the EU." He added that before Finland joined the EU there were many who suffered paranoia that the rest of Europe would come and take away their lands and everything they had worked hard to achieve.

There is a new hierarchy of wealth. The nouveau riche is a new phenomenon in Finland. These are people who have earned money quickly, usually through share options in some of the companies that have become large and successful, such as Nokia. A recent survey showed there are 7,500 people with shares in Nokia worth over one million FIM (US$150,000). Some of these people like to show off their wealth. They buy expensive things because they can afford to do so. This is typically un-Finnish, which is all about modesty and keeping a low profile. Until recently, all Finns thought that if you had something you didn't show it off, because it wasn't good to do so. In a recent survey it was shown that people who won the lottery tended to keep quiet about it. All they did was change their car for a slightly better one. They repaired their houses and they travelled a little more—but nothing too ostentatious.

Although the Finns have built for themselves a sort of classless society, it would be untrue to say that there are no prejudices at all. Indeed, people in the north and rural areas feel that those who live in the big city of Helsinki look down on them. It has only been in very recent years that the Sami people, and their culture, have begun to emerge from under Finnish suppression. These hard-working people from Lapland, who endure the most extreme weather on this Earth, have long been regarded as a slightly inferior race. There is also a small population of gypsies who live in Finland. These Romany people number about five thousand. They are descendants of people who emigrated from India around A.D. 500. They have their own language, culture and dress. The gypsies are often treated with suspicion and have faced discrimination in jobs and housing, and harassment by the police.

There can be very few other industrialised nations of the world that have so few ethnic minorities. Finland gave a home to many 'desirable' refugees—educated people from Vietnam or Kurdistan. With backing and sponsorship from the Red Cross, for the most part, these people were well-received and cared for. However, in 1990, a real problem arose when a group of Somalis turned up at the Soviet/ Finnish border, uninvited, unsponsored and unexpected. Most Finns did not want them to stay. This was little to do with racism but more to do with the psychological difficulty the Finns have with making room for others and to share the hard-earned fruits of their labour.

In 1990, there were only 9,000 foreigners in the whole of Finland, which included one thousand refugees. However, it is estimated that there are now around 80,000 foreigners in the country. What a shock that must be to a nation that has had few visitors from the outside world. Indeed when the Olympic Games were held in Helsinki in 1952, that was the first time that many Finns saw a Negro and the many different races of the world. Foreigners are seen to be oddities. Although the Finns have a very great ability to accept people for what they are and reserve their judgment, their attitude and treatment of coloured people can seem fairly racist. I notice that whenever I go through customs, anyone with a non-European look always spends more time at the customs desk. A black British colleague told me that she found she was often the object of attention and suspicion. According to one Finnish psychologist, the refugee situation is now posing quite a problem in Finland with racism becoming a real issue. That never existed before because there were so few foreigners. Now, a coloured person in the street is assumed to be a refugee. It does not seem to occur to them that the person might be a professor or a business person.

Helsinki

Helsinki, on the other hand, is quite a cosmopolitan town with a multi-cultural society. The small town of Järvenpää, the home of Sibelius, has 35 different nationalities with about 50 different languages or dialects. It has an Orthodox church, a mosque and a Lutheran church and is used to visitors. But the rest of Finland is different. When you travel in rural areas, you will find that as a foreigner, you will be the object of fascination. The locals will take the opportunity to give short stares when they think you're not looking.

However, a passion for equality has been the driving force for the nation of Finland over the last fifty years. They have built for themselves a sort of classless society where living standards are high, and with relatively little difference between the highest and the lowest salaries. High levels of taxation give Finland one of the most comprehensive welfare systems in western Europe, and all this has been achieved by gradual consensus. Employment law is quite rigid and very much favours workers' rights. The owner of a small engineering company explained that his workers were only allowed to work 40 hours a week and 300 hours overtime in any year. They have six weeks of holiday, including all the bank holidays. Thus, to get the work done he and his family had to work all hours! It is extremely difficult to fire someone when they have started working for you. Interestingly, the law in Finland requires all major employers to provide a 'nuclear' bunker, stocked with provisions, water and blankets at their premises, for the protection of their work force in case of an emergency.

SILENCE

I mentioned earlier that extreme chattiness is viewed with suspicion or surprise by the Finns. This is because it is in their nature to be very silent. The Finns are very comfortable with silence. They don't babble or chat. They joke that they are good at being silent in two languages— Finnish and Swedish. Indeed they find no need to fill gaps in conversation with small talk. They have an intense dislike for the noisiness of southern Europeans. The Finns only speak when they have something to say, and this is usually said in a very quiet, calm and succinct way. They always answer questions with minimal information and without expanding on the answer. Many foreigners take this abruptness as an affront, especially as the answer usually comes without a smile!

The Finns are becoming more aware that they are probably the odd ones out in this respect, and they are learning that they have to develop more social skills when trying to deal internationally. The Finns themselves understand that they can have a disturbing effect on foreigners, especially when they are abroad. A client of mine went with her sister on holiday to Rhodes, and while they were there, people in restaurants kept asking them whether they were all right, and whether they were angry. It turned out that the constant questioning was because neither of the girls seemed to be happy or smiling. Compared with the Greeks, they seemed suicidal.

Interestingly, the *Helsingin Sanomat*, one of Finland's premier newspapers, published an article in May 1999 explaining how Finland was going to be taking over presidency of the EU, and that civil servants had to be trained in small talk. This adds substance to the stories that some of Finland's international companies have had to put on training for executives in 'how to show interest' and 'small talk'. If a Finn asks, "How are you?", he's not engaging in small talk; he genuinely wants to know how you are. Many a foreigner has been astonished that a polite introductory conversation with a Finn has led to a detailed description of someone's ailments! The Finns are interested in you as an individual, but they don't need to show this by using small talk. As they say, at –20°C, they just get straight to the point. It seems as though the Finns believe they will lose some of their integrity if they become more articulate. So, to some extent, you have to be a mind-reader. One Finnish friend says she deliberately tries to be controversial with her staff just to stimulate them into communicating with her about the business. As she puts it, "I can't expect to be a mind-reader all the time!" It is important to remember this point in your negotiations with Finnish business people.

Once the average Finn has had a couple of alcoholic drinks you may wonder whether I am talking about the same people. Watch out when they have a party—it's hard to keep up with them. When the Finns get together to socialise, they can become extremely talkative and noisy. They especially like singing, and need very little excuse to start singing some of their old traditional ballads.

In the winter months, many people become depressed and even more silent; they have a tendency to stoicism and quietness. However, in the summer months they go crazy. As a friend of mine, Janne, says, "The Finns put their life on hold during the winter months, and then let up when the light comes."

PERSONAL SPACE

To understand the Finns' need for personal space, you have to realise that until recent modern history, most Finns lived a simple life by fishing, hunting and cultivating their land. With so few people and such an expanse of land, life was very lonely and often the only contact with people were the family that lived with them. These days, the vast majority of the Finns live in towns and cities, but they still remain a 'forest people' at heart. They love to be in close harmony with nature, and it has to be understood that sometimes the Finns just like to be alone. They have no personal need for constant socialising. They have a great respect for each other's personal space, and can regard any unnecessary and irrelevant small talk as an invasion and an intrusion.

Indeed, many times while on an aeroplane, I have seen two Finns sit next to each other. They might nod on arriving and they will nod as they leave, but during the two or three-hour flight they won't talk at all. Above all, the Finns appreciate a calm society where each individual is accorded space and privacy.

A quarter of the population of Finland owns a summer cottage. The majority of Finns have access to one, either through the company they work for or their families. This is where the average Finn goes to get away from it all. The summer cottage or *mokki* is ideally located on the shores of a lake, surrounded by forest. These log cabins usually provide only the most basic of amenities. Normally, there is no electricity or running water, but the two things that a *mokki* has to have are a sauna and a rowing boat. Most Finns don't travel abroad for their summer holiday; instead they spend the time in their lonely log cabins by the edge of the lake. Some people will spend just two or three weeks at the summer cottage, but many will take their family for a long stay, and mum and dad will commute to work. This return to nature is a family affair. The love of the natural environment is common to Finns of all ages, whether city dwellers or not.

A log cabin

HUMOUR

It is said that the Finns rarely smile, and that they appear to be very dour. However, I know lots of Finns, and under their very quiet exterior, they really are quite bubbly and humorous people. The Finns love to laugh and, most of all, they tend to laugh at themselves. Their humour is devoid of cynicism and has a startling frankness about it. Their jokes are rarely cutting or bitchy, but more a laugh about their own national characteristics. They have a natural intelligence concerning their behaviour. Rather than getting overconfident and bullish they tend to self-doubt, and use humour to put themselves down—or put themselves back in their place. Remember, bragging has no place in Finnish behaviour!

Most jokes are told about people from Savo. People in Savo speak in a coded way; they cannot be direct, they are prone to cunning, and their reason is more developed than their emotions. They always want to be the chief, but they are lazy and they work hard at getting others to do the work. However, they have sharp business acumen, and are resourceful when dealing with other people. They are commonly said to say things like, "Well, you can buy it if you like it." or "It might be this way or it might be that way." Cunning and deceit are the two words most commonly assigned to these people and, to top it all, they have a very pronounced accent about which people like to make fun. The Finns especially like to tell jokes about the Swedes and Russians are also on their list of people they pick on.

ECCENTRICITIES

Just so you would know how wonderfully way-out and wacky the Finns are, I thought I would list for you some of the things they get up to in the year:

- The International Ice Swimming Contest which takes place in a different location each year. A hole twenty-five meters long and five lanes wide is cut out of the ice on a frozen lake. The winner is the person who can swim across the fastest!

- The World Wife Carrying Competition takes place each summer in Sonkajarvi. The team consists of a married couple and conventional means of carrying have long since fallen into disuse. This is a game of tactics where the ham-fisted do not stand a chance. Just to complicate matters, there is a water obstacle to overcome.
- The World Mosquito Killing Championship!
- The Kick-Sledge Championship held in Pieksamaki has the holders of the record kicking a sledge for 24 hours and covering a distance of 500 kilometres (311 miles).
- The Anthill Competition—the person who can sit naked on an anthill the longest is the winner!
- Dragon Boat Racing is an annual event in Kuopio
- The Ice Fishing Contest in Joensuu—but no one ever catches very many!
- The enduring Finnish puzzle: For a nation of shower lovers, why are there so many baths out in the countryside and where did they all come from? Apparently when the 'well-to-do' changed their plumbing from baths to showers in the dim and distant past, they threw out their old baths which were then seized by the farmers and used as troughs for their cattle!

RELIGION

There are two official churches in Finland; the Lutheran church and the Orthodox church. They still collect taxes and register births. Nine out of ten Finns belong to the national Lutheran church. This church has about 4.5 million members in 600 communities, and is the third largest in the world. Christianity came to Finland in the twelfth century from both the East and the West. Hence Finland has an Orthodox church of which there are around 55,000 members. There are fewer than 4,000 Catholics, around 1,300 Jews and some 13,000 Jehovah Witnesses. Around 10% of the population have no religious calling, and therefore belong to the civil register.

The reformation of Martin Luther gradually displaced the Catholic church and the first complete Bible in the Finnish language was written in 1642. Nowadays, there are women Lutheran priests, and the church is seen to be quite progressive and building for the future. The church has become very much more popular in recent years. In the town of Nokia, every Thursday evening the church is so full you cannot get more people in it. People are turning to the church for security and as a way to help them cope with the enormous changes that are taking place in their lives. Well-known fashion models tour the country giving speeches and the church is especially giving its attention towards young people.

Easter is the most important religious celebration in Finland. People flock to religious concerts, passion plays and religious services. Finns like to make the most of this holiday.

Christmas Eve and Christmas Day are mainly family celebrations. This is not the time to get drunk to enjoy yourself. Almost everything is closed and if you are on your own, this is not a good time to be in Finland. The main Christmas meal is served on Christmas Eve, probably at about six o'clock in the evening, after the afternoon visit to the graveyard. This is a very special occasion when the Finns will take candles, light them and place them on the graves of their lost loved ones. The cemetery will be all alight; the light from these flickering candles enhanced by the whiteness of the snow. They may also attend mass. The exchange of gifts and feasting will be saved for Christmas Eve night. The whole family will probably enjoy a Christmas sauna together before partaking of more food.

It wouldn't be right to end the chapter on religion without a mention of the rich tradition of folklore and the old Finnish gods of ancient stories of the nation. There was Ahti, God of Waters and Fish; Väinämöinen, God of the Seas; his brother Ilmarinen, God of Winds and Storms; Tapio, God of Forests and Ukko, God of Growth, Rain and Thunderstorms.

ATTITUDES ABOUT LIFE

The Finns are an extremely conscientious and industrious race. It is part of their national pride that they work hard and study seriously. On the whole, they have a very great respect for education and training and are always working towards long-term good, rather than short-term gain. If there is a job to be done, they just get on and do it with no distraction of small talk. I know a management trainer who has worked in various parts of the world. He claims that the Finns are the only people he knows, where he can give them an exercise to do, return in fifteen minutes and find that the exercise will be completed.

This is an example of how the Finns stick to the rules. They are extremely law-abiding; they are honest and have integrity. You will not be cheated out of any change. Similarly, they do not expect you to cheat them. A good example of this is that no one will check before you leave if you have drunk anything from a hotel minibar. I queried this once and the lady receptionist just turned and said to me, "We trust you." You don't have to wear your handbag padlocked to your side, and if you were to leave your wallet in a restaurant it would, more likely than not, be returned intact. This relatively safe-from-robbery environment does not mean to say that the Finns take this for granted. They do secure their personal belongings and lock their doors. On the whole, Finland is a country where you can walk safely at night and be safe from personal attack. There seems to be a sort of invisible authority that rules the lives of the Finns. This is certainly not due to a heavy-handed police presence. As one French friend of mine said about Finland, "I don't think I've ever seen a policeman in Finland, so I couldn't describe one."

This national trait of obeying the rules means that their moral and ethical code is very black and white. The Finns have only been in the EU for a few short years, and yet they are already discovering that if they want to survive, they are going to have to learn to bend the rules, just like everyone else. However, this does not sit happily with them. The Finns have a highly developed civic sense. As individuals, they act as they wish, as long as it is not against the common good. They are self-sufficient and independent, and keenly respect the rights of others to be independent. They value their freedom and their personal space intensely. However they also realise that they have to take responsibility for this total freedom. Interestingly, one Finnish opposition party is suggesting that, should they be elected to power, they will reduce the tax burden on the ordinary Finnish citizen. This is not proving to be a popular and winning election policy, as the majority of the Finns believe this will increase the gap between the 'haves' and the 'have nots.' Their deep-rooted sense of fairness and their belief in looking after those who are less fortunate than themselves means Finland is a country where few have too much and fewer have too little.

The Finns are pretty tolerant of odd and different people and habits. Foreigners are still a pretty rare commodity in Finland, and rather than being viewed with suspicion, they are viewed with interest. The Finns are very open to new ideas, and will soon adopt, adapt and improve any concept or thing imported from abroad. Finland has become known as a very accommodating and profitable place to do business.

Some Finns still find it difficult to share or set up partnerships; this is due mainly to the fact that the Finns like to be independent and self-sufficient. They can view with suspicion partnerships and cooperations where they believe others may try and take away their hard-earned gains. If you work for a Finnish firm, and you are not Finnish, don't expect a promotion. It seems very difficult for the Finns to give that to a foreigner. Some of the large international firms in Finland are beginning to learn that they need to bring in foreign advisors and different international expertise. They have recognised that in this international and global economy, they must embrace their foreign workers as valued, trusted and permanent members of their companies. This is not the easiest thing for them to do. One consultant I met was working on a project for a newly merged Finnish/Anglo/German company. She was doing an audit of the skills and qualifications of the work force. She soon found that a number of foreigners were leaving after reaching middle management because they were not native speakers of Finnish and perceived they had reached a 'glass ceiling'. When the Board were confronted their response was, "After all, we are a Finnish company."

I keep hearing little stories about Finnish jealousy from the Finns, and I'm told that they are a jealous people: "In the west of Finland they try and keep up with the Jones and in the east they try to take away what people have got!"

ENVIRONMENTAL CONSCIOUSNESS

I cannot emphasise enough that the hearts of the Finnish people lie in the lakes and the forests. As a race, the Finns really do care about their environment and the defence of nature; especially the lakes which are high on their political agenda. There is an on-going battle to save the country's greatest assets; their lakes and their forests. As early as 1886, the Forestry Act was passed to curb the wasteful use of forests. In the early days of independence, the republic introduced legal protection for the forests and threatened species. Nowadays, there are strict conservation laws and everyone is encouraged to take individual responsibility for the protection of their wild life. Green policies are part of everyday life in Finland. There is an on-going research to improve house insulation. Recycling schemes are the norm and not the exception, and the government is committed to ever better public transport. Petrol sold in Finland is unleaded.

The Finns have recognised that they are living with a fragile harmony. Their will to preserve what they cherish above all else is almost without parallel. Their concern to do right by their natural environment is deeply anchored in their beliefs. Recently, the Finns have become aware of the detrimental effect the salt that they sprinkle on the roads in winter is having on the watercourses. Research for a better substitute is now underway.

Forests cover 78% of the total land area of Finland. These forests have always been an extremely important source of the wealth of Finland. This is the country's largest resource and major export. Potentially, forestry, timber processing and mining can do the greatest environmental damage. However, these industries add up to a considerable portion of the country's income.

About three-quarters of the forests in Finland are owned by ordinary private families. All forest owners are under legal obligation to replace anything they cut down. So it is in everybody's interest to maintain healthy forests, and trees are carefully managed and harvested. Sustainable forestry is high on the political agenda. Protected zones now account for one-third of the area of Lapland and there are thirty national parks and nature reserves. These areas have been created to encourage natural forestry; this means there is no extensive tree felling, few roads and natural regeneration.

Forests are also an important source of recreation in Finland. There is a law called 'Every Man's Right' which means that anyone is allowed to pick berries and wild mushrooms in any forest, private or public. This right of access is an important part of Finnish traditions, as the picking of berries and harvesting of mushrooms is a national summer pastime.

To the outside world, Finland still represents a supremely unspoiled environment. However, Finland has its problems. It was the first western country to notice the disastrous effects of the Chernobyl catastrophe. This meant that hundreds of reindeer had to be slaughtered. It suffers from air and water pollution arising from the activities of its Russian neighbour. Poland and East Germany contribute to the pollution of the Baltic Sea. By comparison with some areas in Europe which are really polluted, Finland is relatively unspoilt. However, the country is aggressively pursuing energy conservation policies, trying to limit the despoliation of its natural landscape and trying to create new and environmentally friendly waste management systems.

All these initiatives have meant that the Finns have developed a great deal of expertise in environmental matters. They have offered their technological know-how, and clean air and clean water industrial technology to their neighbours, Russia and Eastern Europe, in the hope of slowing down the pollution process.

Even the national anthem, and the blue and white flag of Finland, are tied up with the people's love for their landscape. The national anthem was written to celebrate the country's summer landscape, while the flag is supposed to represent the white of the snow, and the blue lakes of summer. Literature, fine art, design and architecture are all expressed in terms of their environment.

Good design is a passion among the Finns. Although their design can be put under the generic term of 'Scandinavian' or 'minimalist', the Finns have created their own style. This style has had many threads of influence. Traces of the original Byzantine designs that came with eastern invaders can be seen in the rich geometric designs. From Sweden came designs originating from the west. There has been a strong heritage handed down from traditional textile art which can often be seen on their pottery, textiles and interior decoration. On the whole, Finns prefer natural products, but they bring together both natural and artificial products in a way which stamps modern Finnish products with a unique character. Whether creating a product for glassware or textiles or industrial design, the Finns pursue their obsession for things to be of aesthetic beauty. The Finns long ago discovered that good design was not only something that was aesthetically satisfying but also commercially profitable.

HOLIDAYS

The Finns traditionally get about five weeks paid holiday a year, plus public holidays. Usually, the time they take off during the summer will be spent at their summer cottage or enjoying the long daylight hours of midsummer in Finland. A winter skiing holiday and a trip to sunnier climes will be built around the other weeks. One warning to foreigners who may be tempted to come to Finland to join in some holiday festivities is that the Finns themselves tend to leave the cities in droves and everything is closed: hotels, restaurants, museums etc. You may be able to find a small family hotel, which will be open, but unless you have Finnish friends to spend time with, there will be nothing for you to do. Alternatively, you can stay in one of the increasingly popular holiday villages which have built-in entertainment.

The most important holidays in Finland are Easter and Christmas. Easter is a Finnish version of Halloween; children dress up as witches or trolls, with trick-or-treat style traditions. The doorbell rings and you are reminded that it is Palm Sunday when you open the door and see three girl-hags clad in shawls and clutching pussy-willow twigs adorned with pink and yellow feathers. "Give us coins or candy," they shriek. The Easter chicken delivers Easter eggs during the night when children are asleep (just like Santa Claus with his presents at Christmas time) and the children experience the same wondrous excitement. People paint Easter eggs and eat *pasha*, an Easter custard, and *mammi*. *Mammi* is an exclusively Finnish seasonal cake made of rye and malt, that goes well with cream and a sprinkling of sugar.

A Christmas fair

71

Midsummer is also of especial importance to them. This holiday celebrates the longest day of the year. The festivities always take place on the Friday night and Saturday between 20 June and 26 June. The Finns leave the towns en masse to spend midsummer in the countryside. There is usually a midsummer festival full of music, dancing and food; and a gigantic traditional bonfire is lit.

May Day, on the first day of May, is another holiday. On the evening of 30 April, there are lots of festivities. It is, of course, also International Labour Day. It is traditional at this time of year for people to put on their white student caps—the caps that they wore for (school) graduation day. It is quite common for decorations to be put up a day beforehand, even in offices. This holiday is spent eating and drinking. It is definitely a time for partying and a great deal of fun.

Another bank holiday is Independence Day, which falls on 6 December. This is always a sombre and serious day to mark Finland's independence from Russia in 1917. Independence Day is a time when Finns like to eat a festive lunch in a restaurant with relatives and friends. People light candles and put them in their windows, and then they visit cemeteries and light candles there. In the evening of Independence Day, the President of Finland always holds a huge formal party for all the VIPs in Finland. This party is televised and becomes the highlight of the holiday.

The Finns celebrate their New Year the same way many in the rest of the world do with speeches, fireworks, partying and making New Year resolutions! Although not a public holiday, 5 February (Runeberg's Day) is another day to celebrate. This is the national poet's day when people eat a traditional regional cake. Finland has sixteen flag-raising days—six of them official and ten unofficial. On official flag days, government institutions are obliged to fly the flag. Spring is known as the high season for flag-raising which begins with Agricola's Day (the father of the Finnish language, 9 April), Veteran's Day (27 April), May Day (1 May), Snellman's Day (the father of the Finnish currency and a senator and statesman in pre-independence

Finland, 12 May), Mother's Day (14 May), and Remembrance Day (21 May). Other occasions are the Finnish Defence Forces Day (4 June), the Day of the Finnish Flag (24 June), Eino Leino's Day (a famous Finnish poet and writer, 6 July), Aleksis Kivi's Day (author and poet, 10 October), United Nation's Day (24 October), Swedish Day (6 November), Father's Day (November), and Independence Day (6 December). The new year kicks off with Runeberg's Day (5 February) and the Kalevala's Day (the national literary epic, 28 February). Only two of the flag-raising days are public holidays: May Day and Independence Day.

Public Holidays in Finland

1 January	New Year's Day
6 January	Epiphany
March/April	Easter including Easter Monday
30 April	Evening—May Day festivities
1 May	May Day
May	Ascension Day
May/June	Whitsun
3rd weekend in June	Midsummer Holidays
1 November	All Saints Day
6 December	Independence Day
24-25 December	Christmas Eve and Day
26 December	Boxing Day

Further information regarding Finnish festivities can be found on www.festivals.fi or Finland Festivals (09-621 4224) info@mail.festivals.fi.

DRESS CODE

The Finns are very casual about dress code. If you see a Finn wearing a dark suit, white shirt, and a coloured tie, he is probably not Finnish, or he is Finnish, but in another country! Finnish managers may wear trousers, jacket, shirt (and tie) for work. This is what they call 'city wear'. A suit is for 'Sunday best', for big family occasions, or business visits in foreign countries. A large proportion of men will wear jeans and a jumper. In winter it is quite acceptable for managers to wear polo neck sweaters under their jackets and be accepted as smart. There are no hard and fast rules about what you should wear. In summer, Finnish men tend to wear lovat-coloured jackets. Although these are colourful, they are not bright. However, they are a blend of colours which is almost unique to Finnish fashion.

Women dress casually, too. It is more usual to see women wearing trousers than a skirt; topped with a jumper it is quite acceptable for work and is far more casual than you will find in the UK. In summer, a cool cotton summer dress works fine. On the whole, Finnish women wear very little make-up, and hardly ever wear coloured nail varnish.

There can only be few places in Finland to visit where you feel the need to look ultra smart or particularly glamorous. The Finns will accept you however you are dressed, and judge you little by your appearance. A French colleague of mine felt quite insecure when she first came to Finland. The Finns would avert their gaze from her, and she was quite sure that something disastrous had happened to her appearance. Nothing of the sort had taken place. It was just that the Finns rarely engage in eye contact, and even more rarely express an opinion about somebody's appearance. It is very unusual for anybody to pass comment on a pair of earrings, or a dress, or a nice pair of shoes. This tends to make you think that they just don't notice. However, I think it all boils down to the fact that Finns don't engage in small talk, and probably feel it would be very intrusive to make personal remarks. Anyway, the Finns are very pragmatic, they take you for who you are, not for how you dress.

It does seem that the vast majority of Finns prefer to conform in their manner of dress, which emphasises their national trait of not wanting to stand out from the crowd. It is also possible to see long-haired, pony-tailed men; people in outrageously coloured outfits; or even the odd hippie walking the streets. However, these occasions are very rare. In Helsinki you can see beautifully made-up women in designer outfits but I get the impression that there is no pressure to compete. For the handful of women who are dressed like this, there are hundreds that are not. Generally speaking, clothing for the Finns is practical; it's what they use to cover themselves up and keep themselves warm.

So, if you're travelling to Finland, what sort of clothes do you need to take with you? Layers of clothing work best, at any time of the year. As I was advised when visiting Lapland in midwinter, you really need nothing more than your normal city/town wear. A layer of long woollen underwear is needed for the winter as well as gloves and caps and hats. Never forget that the Finns have very efficient central heating systems so the need to dress warmly when you're indoors is not a necessity. One Finnish friend said she has piles of woollen jumpers in her cupboards given to her by foreign friends. Unfortunately, unless she travels to the Mediterranean in the winter time, she says she never has occasion to wear them in Finland—it is too warm! If you wear a jumper you might find that you are too warm when you work indoors all day. However, the danger comes when you step outside.

Never underestimate how cold the weather can turn. If you know that you are going to spend any length of time outdoors, ensure that you have warm underwear on, thick trousers and a thick sweater—just for starters! To top this, an extra sweater comes in handy, but a must is a very thick and long winter coat. A scarf, woollen cap and mittens or lined gloves are also essential. However, for those who spend little time outdoors and are just travelling from home or office, in a car or a taxi, normal city wear is what most people tend to wear. This is topped by their very warm, thick, winter coat and, as always, a woollen cap, scarf, mittens and good shoes!

One of the essential items that you will require when you go to Finland, is a pair of lined and waterproof boots. If you are going to spend any length of time in Finland, or indeed visit Finland quite

What to wear in Lapland

regularly, I would recommend that you buy your boots in Finland. The boots are made to withstand the weather in Finland. They are usually thick soled to prevent the cold coming up through your feet, with good grips to prevent you from slipping on the ice. They are lined to stop your feet from getting cold from above when you step into snow, and most importantly they are waterproof. The boots are far less expensive than in many European cities and are tailor-made for the purpose. Winter boots and winter shoes are subjected to clever Finnish design, which means that they can be extremely smart, and you would never realise that they are such practical footwear. They can appear very chic.

The summer can be hot and humid! Cool cotton summer-wear is a must. However, warm clothes and a waterproof and wind-proof jacket can also be essential. In Britain, we say that we can experience four seasons in any one day. Finland isn't any different! Just as good waterproof shoes/boots are an essential part of winter life in Finland, very good sunglasses are an essential part of summer in Finland. Even in Finland, on a sunny day, twenty-two hours of sunshine can make your eyes very tired. From March onwards, sunglasses are needed. The spring sunshine reflecting off the snow means that the day can be unbelievably bright.

It's very usual in Finland to have outdoor shoes and indoor shoes. In winter most people wear their boots and go to work carrying their indoor shoes in a bag. Open-toed sandals worn with or without socks are always in vogue. One of the things I have noticed is that people often take their shoes off indoors and in public. On the aeroplane, in training rooms or even in business meetings, shoes will be slipped off, without any self-consciousness. Obviously, this seems to be acceptable behaviour—but don't try it in Britain!

So, what happens when people go out at night? I have been to a few informal occasions, such as barbecues, and have found the Finnish men rather formally dressed compared with what I would expect to find in Britain. I am told that open-necked tee-shirts or polo shirts would be the norm, but I haven't seen them being worn. Although very few restaurants insist on men wearing ties, at most of the restaurants I've been to, I've seen men wearing them. However, I do make a distinction here between restaurants and fast-food or chain restaurants. Women especially like to dress up, and I have seen some ladies turn up in wonderful evening wear for special occasions. (They arrive in their boots with their best shoes in a bag, and change on arrival.) The local midweek dance is a time when everyone tries to look smart—without 'dressing up'.

The overwhelming impression I have of a Finnish dress code is that people dress to suit themselves. This tends to be very pragmatic and sensible with nothing making themselves stand out from the crowd. Jewellery is minimal, though exquisitely designed.

PHYSICAL CHARACTERISTICS

The Finns are the darkest of the Nordic races. Finns who are descended from the Swedes are taller, slimmer, fairer and sometimes blonde. Other Finns, descended from the eastern Europeans, are shorter, stockier, dark-haired and brown-eyed. There have been few refugees and immigrants over the years. Thus, Finnish stock has been little diluted by other influences.

Personally, I haven't found a typical Finnish look. The one physical trait I notice is that the Finns have extremely baby-fine hair (apparently this is very difficult for hairdressers from other parts of the world to cut) so many Finns wear their hair short. Finns have finely pronounced cheekbones. They may be heavy-browed and usually with small eyes that are generally blue or slate-grey. On the whole, the Finns are either slim or of medium build. It is very rare to see anyone who is obese and only a few are overweight. Heart disease is reckoned to be a problem in Finland, especially in the eastern region called Karelia, where a lot of their traditional food contains cream, butter or milk. Even there, obesity is a rare sight.

Chapter Five

LANGUAGE
AND LITERATURE

Another of the fascinating contradictions you will encounter in Finland concerns its language. As previously mentioned, Finland has two official languages: Swedish, which is spoken by about 6% of the population and whose presence came about through 700 years of Swedish supremacy, and Finnish. Yet, Finnish is both old and new. As a spoken language, Finnish has existed for years and was thought of as the language of the common people. It was only in the Middle Ages that Finnish was written down, when Mikael Agricola created the first Finnish alphabet in 1543. Hundreds of years passed before Finnish was elevated to the status of a true, written, cultural, and official language. This was in 1863, when Finnish was given parity with Swedish as a national language. Until then, Finnish folklore was an oral tradition and early literature was written in Swedish, with more scholarly work in Latin. In modern times, the Finns have found knowing foreign languages essential to their economic wellbeing. Much time is spent on learning languages in Finnish schools, with

English being the most popular foreign language. The vast majority of Finns use and understand English in their business transactions and many speak German and Russian.

THE LANGUAGE

The early inhabitants of Finland were thought to have come from the Ural mountains in Russia and they brought with them a language which belongs to the Finno-Ugric group of languages, part of the Uralian family of languages. Other related languages in this family are Estonian, Hungarian, Lapp and several lesser Russian languages spoken by minority groups. These languages have been around for thousands of years. Finnish was established in the geographical region of Finland around 3,000 B.C. While Hungarian and Finnish are thought to be related they have developed separately over the last 6,000 years, and are now quite dissimilar.

Today, Finnish has numerous words borrowed from its many neighbours which demonstrate millennia of contact and interaction between its peoples. An Indo-European influence has been gained through Baltic, Germanic and Slavic languages. More Finno-Ugric influence was borrowed through Estonian and the other Balto-Finnic languages of Karelian, Ludic, Veps, Votic and Livonian. However, modern-day influence has come especially from Swedish, with Germanic and Scandinavian languages making a contribution. Although Finnish may have many words borrowed from other languages, its ability to absorb these into the language in a unique Finnish way makes them almost unrecognisable as 'foreign' words. Coffee, for example, is *kahvi* and bacon is *pekoni*. The language is still being consciously developed and due to a flexibility within the language that allows you to 'glue' words together, (Finnish is an agglutinative language) international words are kept to a minimum. Whilst television is *televisio* in Finnish, computer is *tietokone* (knowledge machine) and telephone is *puhelin* (to do with speech).

I was amazed when I first heard Finnish spoken all around me. The image I conjured up was of Italian. The language sounded so melodic, so soft and so pretty. Others have said it sounds like Welsh. It seemed as though every word ended in *i* or a vowel, which gave the impression of people singing. In fact, within the grammatical structure of the language there is a rule concerning vowel harmony, thus distortion does not appear. The most common sound in Finnish is the vowel *a* and the least common is the *ö*.

The Finnish alphabet has three extra letters: Å, *ä* and *ö*. The language is phonetic, where every letter in a word is pronounced. Any adopted words from a different language will be adapted to fit into the Finnish phonetic system. Vowel harmony can also affect some grammatical structures. So that pronunciation is clear, Finnish uses double letters as a distinctive feature. Thus, all eight Finnish vowels *a, e, i, o, u, y, ä, ö,* and many consonants may appear in writing with two letters to denote a long sound and one letter for a short sound. An example of this is *kukka* meaning flower and *kuka* meaning who.

Finnish has a fearsome reputation for being impossible to learn by adult foreigners. However, I am informed that Finnish is very logical. It is not difficult, just different. Personally, I don't agree with this statement! I struggled with German and its four cases, others find Latin difficult with its six cases, so Finnish with 15 cases has to be as near impossible as you can get! To demonstrate, Finnish has a rich system of word flexion which adds suffixes, prepositions and post-positions to the root of the word. Thus, just learning and recognising basic vocabulary becomes exceedingly difficult as so many additions are made to the original form. These additions are used to show grammatical relationships and can express time, place, ownership, object, manner, etc. Finnish is, therefore, thought of as a synthetic language because it can use suffixes to express grammatical relationships and derive new words. One word in Finnish: *talossanikin*, is translated into English as 'in my house, too'. The suffix *–ssa* corresponds to the English preposition 'in', the suffix *–ni* here means 'my', and the suffix *–kin* corresponds to the English word 'too'.

The length of Finnish words can be unbelievably long and usually needs a good few English words to translate. *Kirjoitettuasi* when translated means 'after you had written'. Because each noun or verb has so many additions showing its grammatical relationship, word order in Finnish is far less important than in English. 'Peter hates John', for example, has a different meaning from 'John hates Peter'. However, in Finnish, *Pekka vihaa Jussia* ('Pekka hates Jussi') can also be written *Jussia Pekka vihaa* because the direct object is apparent and it is quite clear that Jussi is the object of the hatred.

There are many features in the language that still show its Uralian origin, for example, the absence of gender. The same Finnish pronoun *han* means both 'he' and 'she'. Often you will find that Finns get muddled, using pronouns interchangeably when speaking English, so you have to listen carefully for a name to work out whether they are speaking about a man or a woman! Also, Finnish does not have the definite and indefinite articles, 'the' and 'a' in English. There is no equivalent of the verb 'to have' and no direct counterpart of the passive verb forms of Indo-European languages. Additionally, in order to express negation, the Finns use a word which corresponds to the English word 'not', but this has to behave as a verb and changes according to the person. Questions can be posed by adding the suffix *-ko* after a verb. Finnish is said to be a very conservative language because it is slow to change and many borrowed words still have their original root. The Finnish word *kuningas* meaning 'king' still has the same word as its root. It was borrowed from the Germanic languages and in other languages has changed its form quite radically through the years; *king* in English, *kung* in Swedish, *konig* in German.

Finnish is a language that you do not just 'pick up'! It seemed to take me forever to remember even everyday words such as 'thank you', *kiitos*; 'yes', *kylla*; and 'good morning', *hyvää huomenta*. As foreigners, our problem is that we have no hook on which to hang even simple information—nothing relative or similar. My experience of learning languages has been confined to European languages, but there is nothing in them to help me master even a modicum of Finnish. So, for anyone wanting to learn the language—best of luck! However, a consistent and disciplined effort will let you achieve huge results, but dipping in and out of learning will leave you none the wiser. The logic and the process of the language structure have been likened to mathematics and studying Finnish can be seen as a similar challenge. I would like to thank my colleague Timo for giving me clear and uncomplicated explanations of his language, though, after three years, I think he is almost giving up on me. A more in-depth overview of the language can be found on www.virtual.finland.fi and www.hut.fi, which I must thank for giving me the overall framework and the examples here.

THE LITERATURE

Until the sixteenth century, Finnish was a language rich in a folklore of songs and poetry handed down through oral tradition from generation to generation. It had no written form until Mikael Agricola constructed a Finnish alphabet. As Bishop of Turku, he researched the old Finnish gods as a means to further the cause of Lutheranism and so began the research of documenting the folklore in a Finnish written form. The Bishop of Porvoo, Daniel Juslenius (1676–1752), is known as the first of many eighteenth century scholars to research Finnish culture, people and language. This was at a time when Sweden was a great power and dominated the political structure in Finland. His work was always in praise of the Finnish people. The language, cultural traditions and the feeling of a distinct national identity owed much to the survival of their oral traditions, which had been passed on for centuries through tales of the supernatural and legendary characters. Juslenius used folk song texts as proof of an ancient Finnish civilisation and his work drew patriotic appreciation from many scholars who followed in his footsteps.

The first detailed account of Finnish poetry—*De Poësi Fennica* by Henrik Gabriel Porthan, was published in Latin in five parts between 1776–78. A study of Finnish folk poetry, it awakened public interest in Kalevala poetry and Finnish mythology. This work laid the foundations for Finland's most significant literary masterpiece—the *Kalevala* by Elias Lönnrot (1835). Although Porthan was interested in history and folklore, he did not write about Finland as a nation. However, nationalistic ideas were beginning to spread through scholarly circles in Finland and were voiced through a literary association set up by Porthan, known as the Aurora Society. Promotion of the Finnish language and culture gave expression to their patriotic ideals. Sixty years after his death, Porthan was recognised as a national hero and a statue of him was erected in Turku.

In 1809, Finland was ceded to Russia after 700 years of Swedish domination, and Alexander I granted Finland the status of an autonomous Grand Duchy of Russia. It was during this period that the awakening of the Finnish Nationalist Movement came about. Research into the rich and authentic Finnish folk culture inspired the national independence movement. Folklore was to play a significant role in the development of a national identity. The period from early to mid-1800s is known as the age of Turku Romanticism. Many university scholars collected and published folklore material but it was one scholar in particular, Elias Lönnrot, who was to set the Finnish world on fire. With a grant of one hundred rubles from the newly formed Suomalaisen Kirjallisuuden Seura (Finnish Literary Society), Lönnrot travelled to Russian Karelia to collect folk poetry. Making several field trips around the Finnish-Russian border, Lönnrot noted in a letter of 1834:

"a desire to organise and unify them [folk poems] awoke
in me, to extract from Finnish mythology something
corresponding to the Icelandic Edda."

During his fifth field trip, Lönnrot met up with a renowned singer who was then aged 65. The singer had learned his songs as a child from his father and had an extensive repertoire. In two days, the singer sang over four thousand lines of poetry to Lönnrot which he captured as the vehicle to narrate his future epic poem, the *Kalevala*.

In the evolution of the Finnish National Movement the most important literary event was the publication of Lönnrot's *Kalevala* in 1835. This was a compilation of the Finnish folk poetry he had researched and which he transformed into a national epic. With its publication, the status of the Finnish language and of Finnish literature was raised. The positive response to the *Kalevala* enabled Lönnrot to expand his work through collections made available to him by other scholars and, in 1849, a new edition known as the 'new *Kalevala*' was published.

> *"I am driven by my longing,*
> *And my understanding urges*
> *That I should commence my singing,*
> *And begin my recitation.*
> *I will sing the people's legends,*
> *And the ballads of the nation.*
> *To my mouth the words are flowing,*
> *And the words are gently falling,*
> *Quickly as my tongue can shape them,*
> *And between my teeth emerging."*

(Kalevala Poem 1, opening lines 1-10, translation: Kirby)

Towards the end of the 1800s the study of Finnish folklore and Finnish culture assumed great importance. It gave the Finns a self-awareness which eventually made it possible to build a political movement and was instrumental to nation-building.

Aleksis Kivi is seen to be the founder of modern day Finnish literature. He penned a book called the *The Seven Brothers* about seven brothers who try to escape education and civilisation in favour of the forest. *The Egyptian*, published in 1945, is a world-class bestseller from the author Mika Waltari. His book depicts the ancient Egypt of the Pharaohs and contains so much detail that, to this day, it is still regarded as a masterpiece. The most widely translated Finnish author is Arto Paasilinna. He writes picaresque novels which are especially popular in France. The titles of his books include: *The Year of the Hare, The Howling Miller, The Forest of the Hung Foxes, Charming Mass Suicide,* and *The Sweet Old Lady who Cooks Poison.* Born in Helsinki, the author Tove Jansson is known all over the world for her books about the Moomin family. These philosophical trolls have become so popular that they have appeared in some 120 magazines and newspapers, and in over 40 countries in children's books and comic strips, and even in a Japanese television series.

FINNISH FOLKLORE AND PROVERBS

In Finnish folklore, the gods were natural phenomena. The gods were seen as Nature herself, respected by the people who in return received respect from the gods. Tapio was the god of forests, Ahti ruled the lakes and waterways, and one of the oldest was Ilmarinen the blacksmith who is said to be older than the skies. He was born at night and was a fully skilled blacksmith by early morning. As the world was completely empty, he made a forge out of his shirt, used his forearms as hammers, transformed his trousers into the chimneys of the furnace and let his knees be an anvil. Ilmarinen then forged the skies and the stars, created the northern lights to add wonder to the long wintry nights, and welded red into the dawn and the sunset. Väinämöinen is a god even older than Ilmarinen and is the ancient sage and hero of the *Kalevala.* He is the god of the seas. At the end of the epic, Väinämöinen leaves Finland declaring that his services will be in great need some day.

Apart from the gods, there was a plentiful assortment of goblins, elves, gnomes and ghouls who would help people, especially if left a treat. It was common to leave these mythological characters grain, milk, or even money to enlist their help.

In medieval times, the Finns were noted for their witchcraft. It was said that any sizeable forest within Europe had a Finnish witch and people would travel miles to take their advice or listen to their soothsaying. They were especially well noted for their love charms!

Several folk sayings have transformed into proverbs as they pass from one generation to the next by oral tradition:

The visitor has two ways, to come and to leave.

Enjoy coffee when hot, a maiden when young.

Rather a summer without a cow than Christmas without a wife.

The truth won't burn in fire.

Each household lives by its own customs.

Behave in the sauna as you would in a church.

Once uttered, the word won't return to the mouth.

Money will buy your way into society, but a horse will take you there.

Envy will kill the fish in the sea.

A cat's delight is a mouse's plight.

Don't jump before you reach the ditch.

He who wants to climb a tree must begin at the bottom and fly when at the top.

The shoemaker's children never wear shoes.

Chapter Six

SOCIALISING WITH THE FINNS

HOW TO BE A GOOD GUEST

The Finns are conscientious workers—they work hard and they play hard! It is an honour to be invited into the home of a Finn, so the first thing to remember is never refuse the offer of a sauna or a cup of coffee!

However, first things first. If you are invited to a Finnish home, take your shoes off—or at least offer to. Remember, the Finns have outdoor and indoor shoes. It is quite normal for people to bring another pair of shoes to change into, especially in the winter.

Dinner parties are not the norm in Finland. If you are invited, go with either some flowers, or a bottle of wine. This would be very acceptable. But the most important thing is to bring an open mind. The Finns assure me that your being interested in tasting their food is what they really want. Finns enjoy being good hosts and give their best.

It is usual in Finland that people come round for coffee, and this will be served with biscuits or cakes. Traditionally, the host had to serve seven varieties of cookies or cakes, as this is what etiquette demanded. Coffee is to the Finns as petrol is to cars, or so they say. In fact, Finland has the highest consumption of coffee per capita, of any country in the world. Entertaining in Finnish homes is mostly about popping in for a short time to have coffee.

DINING OUT WITH A FINN

If friends want to spend a longer time socialising, they will probably arrange to meet in a restaurant for lunch or for dinner. In this case, each person will be required to pay their own bill. The Finns are very particular about this. They won't split the bill just 'down the middle' or by the number of people attending, which is customary in places like the UK. They like to pay precisely for what they have had. As the Finns would say, "I don't like to travel on your wing." In other words, they don't like to be beholden to anybody else. People who don't pay, or are looking for other people to pay for them are called 'wingers' (*siipeilisä*—our equivalent is 'sponger'). This very precise and careful way of splitting bills is the Finnish concept of fair play. They like to pay their own way. As a foreigner, you may well be asked out to dine. In this case you probably will be invited as a guest and not be expected to pay, but do remember that alcohol is extremely expensive. The next time you meet be prepared to pay for your portion of the bill.

Finns never drink in rounds. Everyone always pays for their own beer, and buys it when they want, even when drinking with friends. As a foreigner you often feel obliged to buy a round, but I have heard it said that no-one feels the compulsion to return the compliment!

My French friend, Christine, cannot get over how little importance the Finns seem to give to enjoying their meals. Of course the French like to sit over their meals, sipping wine and debating till all hours of the morning! The Finns, on the other hand, seem to eat as quickly as they can and get up from the table as soon as they are through. Obviously they all have something more important to do! Of course, hardly a meal will go by without half the diners making or receiving a phone call. Incidentally, if you are in a group, once four people have been served at the table you can start eating; you need not wait for everyone to be served.

MODE OF DRESS

If you are visiting very good friends in the summertime, you will normally find your hosts in swimwear and a shirt. Even if you are visiting someone that you do not know very well, you are still expected to dress informally, but fairly smartly. It seems that jeans are perfectly acceptable and expected at an informal gathering. If you are visiting a restaurant with family or friends, then smart casual dressing or jacket-and-tie would be required. Suits are rarely worn. But, whatever the choice of attire, it should reflect one as 'calmly-dressed'.

WHAT TO DO AT A SAUNA PARTY?

Finland is the land of the sauna par excellence. If you do not want to have the sauna, nobody is going to mind. It's quite accepted that women can feel particularly uncomfortable having saunas and then having to do their hair and make-up again. Also, some men feel that going from extremes of temperature, especially in the winter, is not for them. Whether you sauna or not, matters not. So, if you are invited to a sauna party, just relax and enjoy the time spent with your Finnish hosts. In fact, it is quite an honour to be invited.

What happens in a mixed crowd of adults is that the ladies will be asked to enjoy the sauna first, whilst the men socialise and have a few beers. When the women have finished, showered and changed, the men will then take their turn in the sauna. During this time, the women will enjoy their beer or wine and sit and talk. This all sounds very civilised. It is. However, there have been a few startling occasions when I have been with a group of foreigners. It is usual that on coming out of the sauna, people will stand around naked, or wrapped in a towel, to cool off. This might well be at the balcony. This has caused many a scream from unsuspecting foreign guests when they stumble across a group of the opposite sex during their cooling off period!

Once the enjoyment of the sauna is over, it is then time to get on with the eating and drinking. At a conventional sauna party, you will be offered a mixed salad, and a mixed meat and rice dish to accompany this. All these will have been prepared in advance so that the hosts can join in the fun, along with their guests. As an aside, the Finns will shower completely naked along with others of the same sex; so this is no time to be prudish. Take a leaf out of their books and throw your inhibitions away! A family with children under the age of seven will probably sauna together. After that age, the sexes will take their saunas separately.

The typical traditional sauna is a log cabin with windows overlooking a lake. The original type was a smoke sauna heated by a wood-fired stove but now there can be a stove heated by electricity. If you have the opportunity to go out to the lakes and enjoy a sauna, the format of the event will be similar to the above. The difference will be that you are expected to be masochistic enough to have a short sauna, then jump into the cold waters of the lake, before returning to the sauna again. This ritual is repeated about three times! I am assured that the whole process of hot sauna and cold dip is quite invigorating! Be prepared to be whipped with birch twigs, which is said to do wonders for your blood circulation and skin. After showering and changing, food will be served. Often it is sausages grilled in the open air, and washed down with beer—a wonderful way to spend a warm sunlit summer's evening.

A good friend of mine had quite an eye-opening experience when she first visited Finland. Unaware of Finnish traditional customs, she was invited to a meal with a Scotsman and an Englishman, at the abode of some Finnish people who lived in the forest. They first enjoyed sports like archery and shooting. Then, when they arrived back at the house, she was whisked away to have a sauna with the wife of the household, which included 'skinny-dipping' to cool off. Needless to say, being British she was totally out of her comfort zone! When the wife started to whip her with birch leaves and smear her skin with a therapeutic paste, she decided enough was enough. The Scotsman also had a great time, but the Englishman declined to be whipped.

The Finns enjoy their saunas. One of the greatest compliments they can pay you is to invite you to enjoy a sauna with them. Jumping in and out of the lake, having paste smeared over your skin, and being slapped with birch twigs, are all seen as beneficial and invigorating for your blood circulation and skin. This is not to be thought of as torture! The Finns enjoy it—really!

Once, in a remote town in Finland, I ran into a colleague at breakfast. I explained that I was there with two of our other colleagues. As we intended to go out for a meal in the evening, I asked if he wanted to join us. He replied that his wife's family lived near by and that he had been invited to spend the evening "having a sauna with my mother-in-law." To the English, this sounds quite heroic, but it is quite common in Finland.

FLIRTING

Many who are used to the overt ways of flirting in the Mediterranean countries, think that the Finns don't flirt. They do—it's just done in a very different style. As I have been told, if Finns are flirting very openly, it's usually because they are drunk. Flirting in Finnish is coded in the speech. And in the look. It is direct, frank, short and simple. It would appear that Finnish men never go for a long seduction game, and never bother to use flattery. Many foreign women see this as a bit of a put down, and certainly a put off! One Finnish man promised to write me an 'interpretation guide for foreign women'. This has not yet been forthcoming but, so far, has led to an understanding of the following:

If you're at a dance and a man says to a woman, "Shall we go, or shall we dance?", the interpretation is the equivalent of a man saying to a lady that she is the most beautiful creature that ever walked on God's Earth. This also allows you to cut out the first three or four dates and arrive at the same point in time! One Finnish lady said this was the Finnish men's concept of equality but that somehow it had lost its politeness and finesse.

The Finns often joke at their inability to express their feelings. There is the story told of old Seppo who was sitting at the breakfast table reading the paper, when his wife came down the stairs looking rather disgruntled. Eventually the old wife says, "Seppo, do you love me?" He replies, "Pirkko, I remember the day 40 years ago when we got married. I told you then I loved you. If anything changes, I'll let you know." Then, there is the story of Juha meeting Johanna at a dance. They leave together and he says, "Your place or mine?" She replies, "Why are you talking so much?"

However, in terms of manners at social occasions, the Finnish ladies do not realise how lucky they are! Without equivocation, I can say that etiquette is alive and well and living in Finland. Gentlemen still help ladies with their coats, hold doors open and stand up when they enter the room. Okay—the younger generation may not be so keen, but there are a lot more men, of a younger age, in Finland observing the social 'niceties' than there are in the UK, for example.

DANCING

The Finns love to dance. Even the men! I was dumbfounded when I took my first group of Finns out in London. After a formal black-tie dinner they wanted to go out dancing and we ended up in a discotheque. After arranging the first round of drinks (we were in England, remember!), everyone was soon on the dance floor—ballroom dancing! The native Brits stood aside and let the visitors take over the floor. They were as astounded as I was. At some point, the dancers formed a circle and a man would choose a lady to dance a few bars in the centre of the circle. Then, the lady would choose a gentleman, and so the dance proceeded. When the music was slow, they would dance a rumba; if they could make the rhythm fit, they would dance a tango; and when the music was quick, they danced their humppa. Foxtrots and waltzes were also on their repertoire. I had a great time. I hadn't danced like that since my mum sent me to ballroom dancing lessons as a teenager!

ALCOHOL AND SMOKING

It is said that the Finns like moderation in everything—except alcohol! There are Finns who are teetotallers. There are those who drink socially and in moderation. However, there are also those who keep alive the Finns' reputation for heavy drinking. These are people who drink to get drunk. Any occasion is an excuse for a good drinking session—especially the many festivals they have in the year.

Alcoholism was the scourge of Finland (and other Scandinavian states) and I am told that alcoholism continues to be a major sociomedical problem. There is still a state monopoly in the distribution of alcohol through state-owned Alko shops. Alcohol is extremely expensive and it is quite a popular thing to take a 'booze cruise' to Tallin or Stockholm to stock up on your bottles. Production, importation and advertising of alcohol are strictly controlled. Alcohol is sold exclusively through the Alko stores but light beer can be purchased in supermarkets. Spirits can only be bought by people over the age of twenty; and wine and beer by those aged over eighteen. Nowadays, beer and wine are far more popular than spirits.

In a restaurant or bar, wine is readily sold by the glass in two sizes —small (12 centilitres or cl) and medium (16 cl). Finland doesn't produce grapes; although there are some locally produced wines made from berries, most wine is imported. Beer (Olut) is light-coloured and is sold by its strength. The most popular of this lager-type beer is of medium strength (strength 3) called *keskari* or *kolmonen*. The strongest is IVA (strength 5), or *nelosolut*, with 5% alcohol. The weakest (strength 1) is *mieto* or *pilsneri* with less than 2% alcohol. The size of the drink is either small (*pieni tuoppi*), medium (*iso tuoppi*, 0.3l), or large (*pitkä*, 0.5l). Alcoholic specialities include vodka and flavoured vodkas, and liqueurs made from cloudberries, arctic berries and cranberries. The Finns love to joke about their 'Finnish white wine' called *koskenkorva* (and as a for-eigner you might be caught out on this one!). It may look harmless enough but it has a real kick—it isn't wine at all—it's vodka!

Remember—alcohol is expensive in Finland, so be warned!

To my very great surprise the Finns smoke like chimneys! Or, so it seemed to me when I first went to Finland. It looked as though everyone smoked, whatever their age.

In actual fact, many Finns do not smoke at all; but those who do smoke, smoke heavily. There are strict 'no smoking' laws restricting smoking in public places to a very small, confined space, where the smoke cannot escape and contaminate the environment. It is important to note that you can only smoke in designated areas, and not just any public place. Also, it is no good your stepping outside the door to have a quick 'drag.' You have to be at least five metres away from the building in case there are any open windows. There is talk of restricting smoking on the balconies of private homes. This is not popular as some smokers do not light up in their apartments but go out on to the balcony to smoke.

Chapter Seven

INSIDE A FINNISH HOME

In the English language, the word 'Scandinavian' has come to imply a certain aesthetically beautiful style—very minimalist, modern, stylish and light in colour. Finnish homes can be described as being 'Scandinavian' in style. The décor is usually white or cream walls with a few choice pictures and white built-in cupboards with either white or natural wood skirting and architrave. Light-coloured wooden bookshelves, light-coloured sofas and chairs, and perhaps a leather comfy chair are about the only furniture. Side tables, coffee tables and all the 'clutter' of a British home is kept to a minimum. One theory for this white and minimalist look is that the style has been heavily influenced by Lutheranism. One thing that strikes a foreigner as decidedly odd is that the doors all open outwards on to the passageways (or they do most of the time, anyway)! So, beware as you walk down a corridor.

FLOORING

An apartment or house will be floored throughout with wood, usually of a very pale colour. The floors have a highly polished finish and can be quite slippery. There may be a few rugs scattered about especially in corridors or passageways. The Finns do not like to have carpeted rooms. One Finnish client of mine asked, "How can you live in such dirty houses?" She was referring to the British custom of having wall-to-wall carpeting. In her perception, the houses must be very dirty because the carpets cannot be cleaned thoroughly. To her, the carpets must be full of germs and bacteria.

WINDOWS

One of the things that surprised me most when I first visited Finland was that the windows cannot be opened. Coming from a family where everyone throws open the windows whatever the weather to let some fresh air in, I found this feature extremely irksome. Modern-day windows are usually heavy wooden frames with triple-glazing. There will be a double-glazed sealed unit on the outside, and a single-glazed pane on the inside, usually all within the same frame. Between the units of glass, there may well be a Venetian blind (a great idea—dust free blinds!). The opening mechanism allows the window to be opened by only a few centimetres, just enough for a draught. However, the lounge or living room will usually have large windows and a French door leading to a garden or the balcony. Window curtains in a home tend to be of very thin material, although quite stylish in their design. Curtains are hung for decoration rather than to shut out the light. The Finns value their privacy and do not like to think they may be seen from the outside, so blinds and curtains are important to them.

THE SAUNA

There is thought to be about one million saunas in Finland and no Finnish home is complete without one. Some apartments may have a sauna in the basement of the building for communal use. The sauna in a home may be only the size of a large cupboard fitted into the shower room. Like all Nordic saunas, it is completely lined inside with wood and heated by a small electric heater in a box covered with stones onto which you throw water to produce steam that makes you really sweat. The stove, called a *kiuas*, heats up the special stones. Normally the sauna is warmed until it reaches between 70°C and 110°C. The best material for sauna benches is Aspen wood because it will not become too warm to sit on, even in a hot sauna.

The best way to enjoy a sauna is to shower first, enter the sauna naked, and then just sit and relax and enjoy the steam. The steam makes you sweat and improves your blood circulation. If you want to give yourself a real treat, then get someone to beat you with birch twigs and smear you with the gooey paste! This process is supposed to be really revitalising and good for your blood circulation. The Finns are very vociferous about the benefits of taking saunas. There is an old Finnish proverb that says, "First build the sauna and then the house." The Finns take their saunas very seriously and it is actually part of their social life. Incidentally, the Finns get most upset when they hear 'sauna' pronounced like the name 'Lorna'. Finns pronounce 'sau' the way we pronounce the word 'how'.

Enjoying a sauna

Some Finns like to show off with foreigners by continually throwing water on to the stoves. This of course will produce enough steam to just about cook everybody in there, but they do it just to test the endurance of the foreigners.

HEATING, GAS AND ELECTRICITY

In urban areas, heating is generated by one central organisation that supplies heat and hot water to all the homes. The British translation would be city heating. The old houses might have gas for cooking but these days, nearly everyone has electric cookers with ovens, and built-in grills that are rarely used. Cooking is done mainly on the hob. Most houses have electricity, using 220 volts and the European two-pin plug. Visitors from UK and the USA need plug adaptors for electrical appliances. All weights and measures are in metric. A few homes still use oil for heating, but they would mostly be in the rural areas. Even though homes have central heating, many Finns also have open fires to heat their homes, using wood-fired ovens built at the sides. This is a tradition that adds to the cosiness of the home. One of Finland's growing exports is fireplaces made of soapstone. These are now the 'in' thing to have and are very popular with Hollywood superstars. The fireplaces can be immense but extremely stylish, and stay warm for a long, long time and heat the whole house.

LOOKING FOR A PLACE OF YOUR OWN

Looking for an apartment for yourself couldn't be easier—do it the Finnish way! Look up real estate agents on the Internet! People shopping around for apartments also tend to use the Internet. Most real estate agents have their own web pages showing the apartments and houses that they have for sale or rent, and their price ranges. This gives you a good indication of prices and sizes of homes in the location that you want to live in. Newer apartments are always very well-equipped and include saunas. A two-bedroom apartment will be between 50 sq m and 80 sq m in area. Newer apartments tend to be smaller than the older ones.

A characteristic of Finnish society is that young people choose first to go and live in an apartment in the centre of the town. It is a common dream to own a home, so they usually buy a plot of land and build their own house. Planning permission is needed to build these houses for you will be required to build in harmony with the district. In other words, you obtain permission and then follow the district guidelines. Loans to build houses can be taken out and repaid over ten years. About 70% of people aged sixty-five and more, own their own homes. Younger people rent, but as they get older, they will at some stage decide to buy and build.

A new 'rich' class is now growing in Finland. As a consequence, there are some very costly apartments in the Helsinki region which are acquired as soon as they are put on the market.

TELEVISION

Prime-time television in Finland is from 7:00 p.m. to 10:00 p.m. The programmes reflect the Finns' interest in the news, the economy, and sports. These take up much of the airtime on television. Many also take part in the national ritual of watching the 8:30 evening news. Apart from the news, the Finns enjoy British and American programmes like *The Bold and Beautiful*, an American series, and *Emmerdale Farm*, a British series. On weekend evenings, the programmes change. Often, there may be a crime series imported from England, Germany or the USA, like the *Miss Marple* series from England. Many television programmes in Finland are imported from Britain and the USA and are broadcast in the English language with Finnish subtitles. This explains why the Finns are so good at speaking English. The same applies to children's programmes. Thus, children pick up English from a very early age. I was most impressed when I heard a three or four-year old girl singing 'Postman Pat' on a train.

Political figures, on the news, are always broadcast speaking in their own language.

A Finnish lady friend of mine said that she once heard nothing but sport on the radio all day long. Having said that, many women in Finland are just as keen on sport as the men.

DOMESTIC HELP

It is not common for the Finns to have someone help with their household chores. This is not part of their culture or their tradition. Another reason could be the extremely high rate of pay for cleaners.

However, you can join a 'circle' at the employment office, which sends someone to your home one day per fortnight to clean and tidy it. This is an affordable way to get help because these people are on the unemployment register, and they claim unemployment benefits. So, in effect, this service is subsidised by the government. It is also possible to hire a cleaning company, and you can put the cost of this against your earnings, and claim tax relief on it. The total amount you can claim in a year would be for about five visits from a cleaning company.

– Chapter Eight –

THE EDUCATION SYSTEM

The Finns have a very high regard for education and have set themselves high targets in the field of education. Ninety-nine percent of the country is literate and investment in education is higher than in any other industrialised country, at just over 7% of GDP (Gross Domestic Product). In 1990 a government commission recommended that one of the strategic aims of the country should be to make the Finns the best-educated people in Europe by the year 2010. It also warned that this would call for considerable increases in financial resources.

The number of newspapers and books printed per capita in Finland is one of the highest in the world. The Finns have the highest rate of library-borrowing in the world—9.7 books or recordings per person per year.

PRE-SCHOOL

At the age of six, children go to a pre-school establishment. For one year they learn how to work in teams and to cooperate with one another, as well as a little discipline. It is mostly play with a little education. Although there is an on-going debate in Finland about getting children to attend school earlier, the Finns largely believe in letting children be children. Almost as a whole, the nation believes that children at this age should learn to be themselves, have confidence, and explore their own creativity. By the age of seven, most children can read and count.

SCHOOL

At the age of seven, children start school. This consists of nine levels, and takes them through to age sixteen. In school, they do the usual subjects which most western societies cover. They have to learn Swedish as their first foreign language. In addition to that, they will learn two, or possibly three, foreign languages, and these will be English, German or Russian.

At the age of sixteen, young people will go on to one of two types of school, a high school or a technical/vocational school. Youngsters wishing to go on to university will go through the high school route. They will have up to four years to pass the high school examination, which is the minimum requirement to apply to university. At the vocational schools, youngsters will learn the skills required to prepare them for a job, for example, as a mechanic or a hairdresser. Recently, students in the vocational schools have been allowed to take the high school examination.

UNIVERSITY

Entrance to university is awarded on a point system. Young people who have the highest grades in the high school examination will be awarded more points. However, this will not be enough to get them into university. The universities themselves set an entrance examination, the results of which are more important than the grades achieved when leaving high school. University education is totally funded by the state, and students get a generous grant, although some of them work to supplement their finances. One consequence of such generous state subsidies is that many students sign up for a university education and go beyond a basic degree. The majority of young people sign up for a Masters and it is very unusual for people to stop at a Bachelors. There is current discussion about limiting the course duration to five years.

There are twenty-one universities and colleges of higher education in Finland, with 80,000 students enrolled, and 18,000 new university students every year. These students obtain state grants. State-guaranteed low interest loans, subsidised health care, meals and student hostels are available to most students. The majority of students stay an average of seven to eight years at university.

OPEN UNIVERSITY
In recent years an Open University system has been established for adult learners. This is especially targeted at professional people without a university background and who wish to study for a degree. Prior learning and experience are taken into account, and the adult learner has to complete various modules for the degree. This scheme has been very welcomed.

EDUCATION SUMMARY
- School is obligatory from the age of seven.
- Six years of primary and junior school are followed by three years at secondary level. After that pupils can stay on for a further three years to obtain a high school certificate.
- Half of all young people, of whom 60% are girls, obtain a high school certificate.

- The nine-year comprehensive school (*Perus-koulu*) includes free tuition, books, meals and commuting to and from school.
- Secondary school (*Lukio*) is for three years and is a stepping stone to university.
- The first university in Finland was in Turku, established in 1640. It transferred to Helsinki in 1828 and now has approximately 26,000 students. It is one of the largest in all Europe.
- The state provides Swedish schools in communities where the numbers justify it. Some universities still have split departments in which instruction is given in separate languages.

Chapter Nine

FAMILIES AND WOMEN'S ROLE

It may seem strange to focus on the role of women in this book, especially as Finland is an industrial society, but it would be all too easy for one to assume mistakenly that Finnish women have the same role as most other women in western society. I found a remarkable difference—it was so tangible you could hit me with it! Personally, I see it as near to ideal as can be found in any developed industrial society.

EQUALITY

The Finns acknowledge that in a small nation, the role of women has been important in both agriculture and industry and in supporting both the family and the nation. Thus Finland was the first in Europe to give women the right to vote in 1906. In the nineteenth century, when boys had acquired the elementary skills of reading and writing, they were traditionally taken out of school and put to work on the farms. Girls, however, stayed on to be further educated. Finland has long had equal opportunities as a 'trademark'. The history of the legal emancipation of women began in the 1860s:

1864: Rights to their own property and income.

1864: Marriage laws improved.

1868: Divorce made easier.

1871: Rights to enter university.

1878: First women physicians licensed.

1878: Inheritance laws amended to inherit equally with men.

1880: Emancipation movement began.

1890: Women allowed to teach in educational establishments.

1906: Universal suffrage, the first women in the world to vote along with New Zealand.

1907: First women elected to the Eduskunta—nineteen out of 200 members of parliament.

1916: Equal pay for women in schools.

1919: The new republic embodied the principles of full equality for the sexes.

1922: Formal establishment of the rights of unmarried mothers and their children.

1922: Father's obligation to support children until seventeen years of age and the right of illegitimate offspring to inherit equally with legitimate children.

1924: Complete equality for women within the civil service— this covered issues such as competence requirements, salaries and pensions.

1981: By this time, 64% of students taking university examinations were women.

2000: First woman president of Finland elected.

Finnish women are very proud of being among the first women voters in the world and they are well represented in the Finnish parliament. The part that women play in Finnish public life is far more significant than can be seen in other countries.

There is a long tradition of women at work in Finland, with almost equal numbers of men and women employed. An overwhelming majority of women (71%) are in full-time employment whilst at the same time bringing up their children and looking after the family. Women in Finland do less part-time work than women in Europe. There are many women in business, in forestry, in engineering and in the chemicals industry. There is no culture of traditional 'women's jobs', such as in welfare and healthcare services, as there is elsewhere. Legally, women have a right to equal pay, but on the whole, women earn only about 80% of men's total earnings. For Finnish women financial independence is the basis of equal opportunity and this explains the importance of work to them. Surveys show that 58% of women regard work as significantly important to self-fulfilment. After the war in 1945, Finnish women bore a heavy responsibility as breadwinners and equalled the men in their struggle to make war reparations to Russia. Until very recently, it was quite common for women to remain in agriculture and continue to maintain the family smallholding, whilst the men became the major wage-earners.

The Rural Advisory Centres play an important role in supporting women's efforts in creating businesses. In many rural regions women work from home in isolation, and the centres have helped developed networks, mentoring programmes and an interactive Internet network. One bank in Finland offers a reduced bank rate for women entrepreneurs.

In terms of breaking the 'glass ceiling' Finnish women can be said to be one generation ahead. Whilst many women in western societies stay at home to look after the children once they get married; in Finland, however well-educated the women are, this does not happen. There are many women in Finland who are in their mid-fifties with well-paid and powerful jobs. There are those who have built businesses and sold them successfully; there are those who have climbed quite high on the corporate ladder; and there are those who have become government ministers. In this respect, Finnish women can be seen as pioneers in working life. According to *Statistics Finland*, Finnish women are better educated than the men which allows them opportunities for similar job status. Women also consider the workplace to be a good environment to learn new things and gain training. They have a great desire for self-development.

The nation, as a whole, tries to encourage women to play an even more prominent role at the highest levels. In 1998, only 2% of senior managers were women (four women in the top 200 companies). A third of Finns have a woman as their immediate boss, more than elsewhere in Europe. Women are seen as popular and successful in their role as a boss. They are said to be more supportive and encouraging than their male counterparts, though, apparently, words of thanks and praise are just as few from the female boss! Today, Finland has as its president a woman—Tarja Halonen. One of my clients from Kuopio, a Finn in his late twenties, voiced this opinion in public a couple of years before she was voted in: "The future belongs to women. They are good leaders." If women in western societies want any role models, they need look no further than Finland.

MARRIAGE AND THE FAMILY

As with many western societies, women are putting off getting married until they reach an older age and marriage, when it is undertaken, is more like a partnership between equals.

Most families have no more than two children, and again the women are putting off having children until later. Although the whole responsibility of the family and the home lies on the shoulders of the women, men of all ages share the responsibility of looking after the children (and a few chores). It is quite common to hear even fairly elderly men talking about cooking or cleaning and looking after children or grandchildren because their wives are working. The Finnish housewife still does more chores than the man and just under one third of couples share housework equally. Of women that work, 27% feel that they are neglecting their home because of work.

A young Finnish student I met, who had spent several months in the United States staying with an American family, told me how different life was there. Family meal-time was something that was a real culture shock for her. She was used to her mother cooking everyday and the whole family eating together. "At home," she explains, "I'll go to McDonald's twice a year. When there...twice a week." She found the habit of TV meals and not eating together very strange and remarked that the American mum only cooked twice in the whole time of her stay. In Finland, families still try to eat together, especially on weekends, when traditionally the meal of the day will be served at 2:00 p.m.

As in many Nordic countries, the divorce rate in Finland is high. According to Finnish female friends, Finnish men are not demonstrative at all, and Finnish women are becoming increasingly so. However, very recently things have begun to change and talking about feelings and personal problems, for both men and women, is not such a taboo. Two books have influenced this. The first was written by the wife of former President Koivisto when she went public about her battle against depression. The second was written by Neil Hardwick, a British author famous in Finland for his TV scripts. He wrote about the effects on his life and family of the 'burnout' he suffered, how it made him drop out of his career and abandon his lifestyle, and the long slow journey to recovery.

Family ties and family values are very strong in Finland and this nation has a worldwide reputation for excellence in welfare. There is an intensive pre and post natal care service for mother and child, and Finland has the world's lowest infant mortality rate. The state guarantees ten months of fully paid maternity leave for either the mother and/or the father. This maternity leave can be split between them. Indeed, Prime Minister Lipponen took two weeks off work when his wife had their child. There are modern, state-subsidised, childcare centres for children until the age of six, when they go to school. In recent years, the state has taken on more and more responsibility for family welfare, and currently it has one of the most generous systems of payment for mother and childcare in the world.

Along with Swedish children, Finnish children were found to be the healthiest in all of Europe in a recent survey.

Just over ten years ago, Finland had one of the highest rates of heart disease in the world. As a nation, the Finns decided to tackle the problem. With good education and local medical centres giving advice, Finland has significantly reduced its national health problem. An English friend who works in the Health Care System in Britain, said the Finns brought about this change because they took responsibility for their own health and that of their families. "It is a

National dancing performance during a mid-summer festival. Finns value their traditions and family ties and such celebrations are opportunities for them to spend time together.

different culture," she explained. "They didn't want to be seen as irresponsible. They didn't want to be a burden to the rest of society."

Medical care for the elderly is good and care for the aged is one of the Finns' built-in values. Pensioners are well-off financially even though there are 40% more pensioners than there are adults of working age. Social security payments for the unemployed are relatively generous and include payment for a television licence, newspapers and the telephone, as these are seen to be essential to the education and well-being of a whole person.

Finland is one of the safest countries in Europe for single women to travel. However, it is not usual to see a single woman in a pub, and she may therefore attract some unwanted attention.

It is still common to see women leaving babies in prams unattended. Children make their own way to and from school. They walk, they cycle or they take the public transport. They certainly experience a degree of freedom that is now quite rare in the West—in a society free from the fear of baby snatchers and child abductors!

Just a note—women will find it very difficult to get an appointment at the hairdressers because appointments are made ages in advance!

FINLAND'S FIRST WOMAN PRESIDENT

Tarja Halonen was voted in as president at the beginning of 2000. A Social Democrat with an intellectual humanist approach to life and the desire to find practical means to improve the society around her, she is called a 'pragmatic idealist'. She is probably the most left-wing head of state the nation has ever had.

She was born and bred in Helsinki, though she lived on the 'wrong side of the tracks' in an area that is considered to be very working class. As a girl she suffered a serious speech impediment, which still affects her slightly even today. She grew up learning to be tolerant and sensitive to the 'differences' of others—especially those less fortunate than herself. She has always had a lifelong interest in human rights

113

and minority issues, and has played an active role in many civil rights associations.

Tarja Halonen began her career as a trade union lawyer, was appointed as a parliamentary private secretary in 1974 and then accepted a junior ministerial position in the eighties. She became Foreign Minister in the government of Prime Minister Paavo Lipponen. Her traditional leftist views are in stark contrast to those of Prime Minister Lipponen, whose political ideology leans more towards a market-led social democracy. When elected president at the beginning of the year 2000, she resigned her party membership as is customary in Finnish politics.

Currently, Finland's Speaker of Parliament and the newly appointed leader of the opposition party are both women.

Chapter Ten

THE CUISINE

Traditional Finnish food is a blend of European, Scandinavian and Russian cuisine, but modern-day food has a strong international flavour. It is said that traditional foods are still those of their Bronze and Iron Age ancestors, namely salmon, reindeer, rye bread, dill, highly aromatic berries and beer. According to the *Kalevala*, the Finnish national epic, Finns in the Iron Age enjoyed frosty, foaming beer. Finland has the oldest breweries in Scandinavia. And for Finns living abroad, rye bread and salted herring are the two things that they miss the most.

A friend of mine related the story about the time she worked with a Finnish trade delegation. She said that whenever they entertained foreign visitors, the menu would always be *gravlax* (a delicacy of cured salmon), followed by reindeer as the main course, and ice-cream and cloudberries as a dessert. Occasionally the menu would be changed to smoked reindeer as a starter, followed by poached salmon for the main course. She lamented that this type of food was served more often than the Finns would actually eat it, for their real favourite is meatballs. At home in Finland, the number one dinner is meatballs and mashed potatoes, with the sauce in the pan made into a thick gravy by adding butter, flour and cream.

The Finns use a lot of cream in their cooking and this is noticeably so in the soups they prepare. 'Cream of…' takes on a new meaning here. Cream of mushroom soup is so thick you can stand a spoon in it, and salmon soup, too, is very rich. You either love it or hate it, and the Finns love it. Many dishes are served with a rich creamy sauce, so it is common to have steak, pork fillet, or chicken breast covered with a sauce that is slightly spicy. Just to ring the changes, you will often encounter a bright red or yellow sauce served with your meat. This sauce is made from berries and I have developed a real taste for this. I have noticed that liver, bacon and mashed potatoes are always served with both a creamy sauce and a berry sauce—the best of both worlds!

Until recently, the only flavouring that was added to Finnish food was dill. Dill is especially used in fish dishes. However, Finnish supermarkets have begun to introduce other herbs and spices and these are now widely used in the preparation of meat dishes.

So, what are the other dishes that are eaten daily by the Finns? Sausage (*makkara* in Finnish) has to be next on the list. The Finns eat makkara and drink beer with a passion. This sausage is more similar to a frankfurter than a British sausage, and is very tasty. Often cooked on bonfires in the open air, makkara is the favourite food for a summer night at the summer cottage. The first time I ate this Finnish sausage was after an afternoon of snow-mobiling in the spring. A group of us snow-mobiled over the frozen lake near Kuopio, around the little islands offshore and alighted on an island that was completely out of sight of civilisation. The sun was just beginning a gradual descent and the sky had turned a magnificent colour of gold and red. Awaiting us were a roaring fire, a crate of beer and a stack of makkara ready for cooking. After the exhilaration of snow-mobiling and the fresh air, we were ready to eat. How good those sausages tasted!

At home, sausages are often eaten and sometimes, cheese is placed in the middle of them and then they are warmed slowly in the oven. Mashed potatoes is the Finns' staple diet but until recently, few vegetables and salads were consumed. Bread is also a staple commodity in the Finnish diet. It seems wrong to me to call Finnish bread a commodity, as that seems to demean it. There are many delicious types of bread and it is said that nearly every village has its own recipes. Like the Italians, the Finns love mushrooms, and there is a real appreciation for all the different varieties that can be picked wild in the forests. A usual week's shopping trolley will have lots of milk products such as yoghurt, milk, *viili* (Finnish yoghurt) and cheese; and cold cuts of meat and sausage. The Finns are fond of casseroles and stews. *Pirro* stew is made with reindeer and potatoes, while Karelian hot pot, *lapskoussi*, is made with veal, pork, mutton and vegetables. *Sekali* is a heavy stew made of pork, beans and sauerkraut.

Cooking makkara in the open

Lunch may be a smorgasbord. The Finns mostly prefer fish and seafood courses. The best restaurants have an incredible variety of food to choose from. The Finnish way to eat a smorgasbord is first to help yourself to the fish dishes, then to take a clean plate and help yourself to the cold meats. After that you can continue with the warm food and follow on with dessert.

Some of the many traditional dishes in Finland are:

- Karelian pie. This is a small pie whose crust is made from rye. It is shaped like a moccasin with a 'ruffled' edge along the top. Filled with a rice mixture, it is delicious served in the traditional Joensuu manner spread with butter and chopped egg. It is served for breakfast, lunch or dinner.
- Kalakukko. This 'fish pie' is a well-known delicacy from the Kuopio region. It is a loaf-shaped pastry filled with fish and fatty pork. The rye dough is filled with vendace, perch, rainbow trout and pork, wrapped in foil and baked in the oven.
- Black pudding. This is a speciality from Tampere and is served with lingonberry sauce.
- Baltic herring is served in many ways—sweet-pickled; sour-pickled; cold in a spicy, curry sauce; marinated; salted or cooked hot.
- Smoked meats and fish. Smoking is an age-old method of preparing food. Particular favourites are smoked reindeer, lamb and ham. Salmon, of course, is one fish that is often smoked, along with trout.
- Berries. Arctic berries that are popular in Finnish cuisine are the cloudberry (which looks like a golden raspberry but tastes of honey), the arctic bramble, the sea buckthorn, cranberry and the lingonberry. There are cultivated berries, currants, raspberries, strawberries and gooseberries which are especially suited to the colder climate and have a distinct flavour compared with those grown in sunnier climes. These berries are made into jams and sauces, frozen or turned into Finnish liqueurs or wines.

Lingonberry jam is served with meat, especially game and reindeer. It is common to have ice cream served with golden cloudberry sauce. Vodkas are flavoured with these berries and Finnish sparkling white wine is mainly made from white currants. White currants are also used to make fresh, fruity white wines.

• Cheese. Finnish-made Emmental cheese is a favourite and is found all over Finland. It is often exported.

There are two particularly grand occasions for feasting in Finland. First is at Christmas and the highlight is the meal served on Christmas Eve. Mulled wine is served with oven-baked ham, mashed swede and potato, lingonberry sauce, blackcurrant jelly and apple sauce. Traditional Christmas sweets often have prunes in them and Finnish Christmas pastries are filled with prune jam. And Christmas would not be Christmas in Finland without large, spicy gingerbread. The Christmas 'cake' is a beautifully created gingerbread house which sits in the middle of the table as a decorative piece until the time to eat it! In December, restaurants serve a Christmas buffet that includes herring; salmon; smoked reindeer; duck; ham; sausage and cod served with a thick milk-based sauce, melted butter and potatoes.

A smorgasbord

The second occasion is at twelve noon on 21 July. This is the gastronomic peak of the summer and the official beginning of the crayfish season. Until the end of August, crayfish parties will be the vogue. Essential ingredients for a really good party are paper lanterns, a warm August evening, great friends and family, toast and butter, *koskenkorva* vodka and crayfish. The crayfish are boiled in salted water, with sugar and lots and lots of dill.

Thursday is traditionally pea soup day; 5 February is Runeberg's Day when bakeries sell a special cake named after this national poet; at Easter the children look forward to *mignon*, egg shells filled with delicious Finnish chocolate and 1 May is a time to drink *sima mead*, a sparkling Finnish white wine, and eat sweet pastries.

EATING OUT

The Finns have developed a taste for international cuisine, especially Italian food. There can hardly be a village in Finland that does not have at least two pizzerias and there must only be a handful of restaurants that do not offer both pizza and lasagne on the menu! Helsinki is extremely cosmopolitan with its choice of good restaurants, ranging from Japanese to Mexican, and from trendy bistros to traditional farmhouses. The variety is plentiful and, in addition, a multitude of cafés, tea-rooms and bars can be found serving light snacks and delicious pastries. In the other major cities in Finland, the choice of restaurants is not so varied. However, there always seems to be a good Russian restaurant around, along with Greek and Italian food. Chinese food is becoming popular with the Finns, though Chinese restaurants tend to be few.

I suppose it goes without saying that McDonald's has a strong presence in the country. (My daughter took great delight in telling all her friends that she has eaten a Big Mac in the most northerly McDonald's in the world – and has the hat to prove it!) But, not to be outdone, the Finns have their answer to the American fast-food chain.

They have 'Hesburger'—their own home-grown burger chain and the outlets are usually located within a stone's throw from a McDonald's. Apart from hamburgers, another popular fast-food is the hotdog and hotdog kiosks abound.

Service charge and VAT (22%) are always included in the advertised price of food, so there is no extra charge to your final bill. Payment can be made by credit/debit card, however small the bill. Tipping is not customary.

THE COFFEE CULTURE

A surprising fact about Finland is that the Finns drink more coffee per capita than anyone else in the world.

I am convinced that they have acquired this accolade not because they drink more cups of coffee in a day but because the coffee they drink is so strong that you can hang wallpaper with it! However, the Finns have a very long established coffee tradition which started at the beginning of the eighteenth century when coffee first arrived in Scandinavia. It had become so popular by 1767 that the government tried to make this 'unhealthy luxury drink' illegal. But those with money were able to buy it on the black market and eventually the government of the day gave up. By the nineteenth century, the coffee habit had spread throughout the countryside. The wealthiest amongst the population drank it daily but villagers would drink it only during their public celebrations and holidays. Ordinary families soon wanted to have coffee for themselves and so began the Sunday ritual of having coffee after church. Unfortunately, coffee was so expensive that other ingredients like rye, barley, beans, peas, dandelion roots, acorns and chicory were mixed with it to lower the price. But when times were hard and the harvests bad, coffee was the luxury that was given up.

By the twentieth century, coffee was established as the national drink. All kinds of coffee cultures arose and people began to drink coffee with sugar and cream. They also began to buy coffee beans and roast them at home in a special pan called a rannali. In this way, each family produced its own distinct blend of coffee depending on the ingredients they had mixed with the beans. Coffee was in such short supply during World War II that when the container ship, *The Herakles*, arrived from Brazil with the first consignment of 35 tons of coffee in 1946, the day almost became a national flag day. There is a sweet bread called *pulla* that is traditionally eaten with coffee. It contains lots of cinnamon and cardamon. In the old days, the pulla was baked as a large circular bun with a hole scooped out in the middle. When the pulla was served the centre would be filled with all sorts of cookies and biscuits, traditionally seven varieties.

– Chapter Eleven –

TRAVEL

Most people travelling to Finland will arrive by air at Helsinki
International Airport. The first thing that will strike the visitor is the
very well-ordered and civilised society. (The number one thing on my
list of what is great in Finland is the trolleys they have at the airport.
These are miniature versions of the shopping trolleys you would find
in a supermarket. They are just big enough to take a heavy coat and
some hand luggage—excellent! You will find them just as you exit the
aeroplane, right next to the gate.)

Finland can also be reached by boat from Estonia or Sweden, or
on mini cruise-liners which sail straight into Helsinki harbour located
virtually in the middle of the town. Travellers taking the train from St
Petersburg, or other parts of Russia, will find themselves arriving at
Helsinki station, again in the centre of the town.

Helsinki harbour

However you arrive, you will find ready and easily accessible transportation to your next destination. Finland is an easy country to get around and, apart from the USA, I find this the best country in terms of facilities for disabled people.

There is a superb selection of free city and regional maps that are obtainable from local tourist offices. There are also maps of waterways and lakes, trekking areas and national parks, and nineteen different road maps.

VISAS AND DOCUMENTS

If you are a citizen of the Nordic countries of Denmark, Iceland Sweden or Norway, you do not need a passport to enter Finland. Citizens of the EU countries, except Greece, need only either their national identity card or a passport. Other foreign visitors will need a valid passport. You will need a resident's permit for any stay longer than three months unless you are a citizen of the Nordic countries mentioned above. For a stay of less than three months' duration, most western nationals will not need a visa. It is always best to apply for a resident's permit before you leave home. Work permits are required for all foreigners other than those coming from the EU and European Economic Area. Employment must be secured before applying for a permit. For more information, apply to the Finnish Directorate of Immigration (Tel 09-4765 5857), Siltasaarenkatu 12a, 00530 Helsinki; www.uvi.fi

DOMESTIC FLIGHTS

Helsinki Airport has won the International Airport of the Year award. It has a good choice of merchandise for sale in the various shops including a wonderful selection of Finnish jewellery and Scandinavian glassware. If you are shopping for children or want a really unusual present, you can buy Lappish dolls in their traditional dress with reindeer skin coats and brightly coloured hats, or you can buy wonderfully detailed Father Christmas and Mother Christmas dolls. There are plenty of restaurants and cafés selling good quality food at fairly inexpensive prices, compared with other European airports. In the international terminal, there are various lounges for frequent flyers and business-class passengers.

There is no business-class service on domestic flights within Finland, and therefore there is no business-class lounge in the domestic terminal. However, there is a lounge for members of the Finnair frequent flyers club. Unfortunately, many a business-class passenger arriving in Helsinki in transit has found his way to this lounge and been turned away.

The principal domestic carrier is Finnair (though you will find that Golden Air will fly internally to a few smaller destinations). There are flights to all the big cities in Finland but they are routed through Helsinki. This means that it is almost impossible to fly from east to west across Finland. You have to go south to Helsinki first. The smallest aircraft in the fleet is now a Saab 340 and it is used on routes that have few passengers or for late night journeys with only a handful of passengers. Unfortunately, the journey itself will take longer on the small aircraft rather than the normal jets. However, I do have to say that Finnair pilots are the best in the world at landings! So smooth!

Finland offers some of the cheapest domestic flights within Europe. There are almost always discounts, promotions or stand-bys available. For further information call 09800-3466 for free for the Finnair general booking office. If you mislay something whilst travelling, the Finnair lost and found department is at 09-818-5324 and the opening hours are 8:15 a.m. until 3:15 p.m.

Having arrived at your destination airport, you will have no problems travelling on from there to your hotel or place of stay. At the very small airports, you will be asked whether you want a taxi. Whilst you are on board the aeroplane, a taxi will be booked for you. At larger airports, taxis will be waiting outside; alternatively you can catch either the airport taxi or the Finnair bus. At Helsinki airport, the airport taxi will take you to your destination for a fare of 100 FIM (US$15). When leaving, you can book an airport taxi to pick you up. Likewise, at large airports around the country, airport taxis will be waiting to transport you onwards. Airport taxis differ from normal taxis in that they will take up to ten passengers. However in reality there is normally never more than five. The Finnair bus is very reliable and great value for money. You will recognise the coach by the blue and white Finnair logo on the side. The coach ride will cost approximately 25 FIM (US$4.50) to the centre of the town. The drop-off points are usually the main railway station, the main bus station, the centre of town and selected hotels. The Finnair bus operates like a regular bus service so you can catch this bus for your return to the airport. It will make the same stops and will collect you probably one hour fifteen minutes before the flight takes off.

The airports around the country are small, so there is no need to check in hours before your flight. Generally speaking, half an hour before the flight takes off is usually long enough even if you are catching an international connection. When travelling abroad via Helsinki, you can check your baggage right through to your final destination and still check in just a short time before takeoff. In all the time I have travelled with Finnair, I may have got my luggage late, but I have never lost anything. However, one person lost her luggage so many times in one year that she was featured on the BBC's *'Watchdog'* programme.

If your luggage doesn't turn up on the conveyer belt at your destination airport, this is what you need to do. First of all, go along to the Finnair desk which is usually the check-in desk for outgoing passengers. You will need to report how many pieces of luggage you are missing and you will be asked to identify a generic type of case from various photographs. If you arrive in the middle of the day, you will probably find that your suitcase will follow you on the next plane. Therefore, within about three hours you will have it. However, if you arrive last thing at night you should ask for an overnight bag. This bag contains all the essentials: ladies' and gentlemen's toiletries and some clean underwear. If your luggage hasn't turned up by the next day, you can claim compensation by writing to Finnair, and you will give receive 500 FIM, about US$75. Be warned—none of this information will be given to you! You need to know that you can have the overnight bag and that it is your right to claim compensation for a bag that has been lost for more than a few hours.

If your luggage is broken during transit, report this at the Finnair desk on your arrival. There will be some paperwork for the airline to complete. However, you will be given a letter or a voucher to go to a local luggage shop to pick yourself a new case. All you need do is choose a new case and they will exchange it for the voucher without any fuss whatsoever.

TAXIS

The word for taxi in Finnish is spelt *taksi* and is easily recognisable. You will usually find taxi stands at bus and train stations, or in Helsinki, at other central points. It is not the custom to hail a taxi on the street. Taxis can also be booked over the telephone. However, if you book them more than two hours in advance you will have to pay a surcharge of 20 FIM (US$3.00) in addition to the cost of the ride. Taxis are almost as expensive in small towns as they are in the large towns. Unlike in some countries, there is no share taxi service available in Finland, the exception being airport taxis. If you are a group travelling a fair distance, you should negotiate for a good price before you start your journey.

BUSES

According to the tourist board, the bus service covers about 90% of the roads in the country. The buses are generally comfortable, and the service is efficient and on schedule. Apart from the local buses that service the town, there are two other types of service: the intercity service and the express bus service. The intercity service has regular buses that stop frequently at small towns and villages on the way to the next city. The express bus travels swiftly between cities, covering 100 kilometres in less than two hours and 400 kilometres in about six hours. Whichever type of service you take, they all have the same ticketing system.

Each town has a bus terminal. This is called Linja-Autoasema and is generally within walking distance of the rail terminal. Most buses run Mondays to Fridays with restricted services on Saturdays, and on public holidays. Very few buses operate on a Sunday, and bus stations close at 6:00 p.m. Mondays to Saturdays, and 4:00 p.m. on Sundays. If you are travelling long distances, it is usually better and cheaper to travel by rail. However from village to village, buses are the most expedient forms of transport.

For information on long distance and express buses, contact OY Matkahuolto Ab (Tel 09-682701), Lauttasaarentie 8, 00200 Helsinki, or www.expressbus.com.

RAILWAYS

I was most impressed with the Finnish rail service when I first used it on a journey from Helsinki to Joensuu. I arrived at Helsinki station and saw an old vaulted building which reminded me of something off a spy movie set in Moscow. The intercity train, however, was modern, clean and tidy, and travelled quietly and smoothly. There were Pullman seats on first class, but the whole train seemed to be very roomy. The train left punctually and kept to its schedule throughout the journey. The price of a first-class ticket on an intercity train includes food. The restaurant on the train was very cosy and the food was more than adequate. There was also a bar area, rather like a pub. The whole journey was very pleasant and with little hassle. There is just one thing to take special note of: there is a huge step up from the platform onto the trains in Finland. If you have luggage with you, you will need a push-up with it. This really is my worst nightmare when travelling by train in Finland, and I always try to reduce the weight of my luggage when doing so.

On the longer routes, there are sleeping cars available and special car carriers. They will all have dining carriages that serve snacks and meals which are tasty and good value for money. Seating is either in first class with Pullman-type seats, or in second class which are open carriages with soft chairs. Seat reservations are mandatory on intercity trains, and the high speed Pendolino express trains. Tickets can be bought from the guard on the train at a small supplement. First-class tickets are one and a half times the cost of a second-class ticket. Travelling by train is cheaper than by bus. Visitors aged over sixty-five are entitled to a discount on rail tickets if they show their identity card or passport.

Helsinki is the main rail terminus for the south of the country and Rovaniemi is the main northern terminus. There is a fast and efficient service on the north-south route, but this is not duplicated on the east-west route. The trains are fewer in number. There are three main rail lines: the Pohjanmaa line runs between Helsinki and Oulu in the north, and continues to Kemijärvi in Lapland, the Karelian route runs from Helsinki to Nurmes via Joensuu and the Savonian route runs from Kouvola in the south to Iisalmi in the north continuing to Kajaani.

The railway station at Joensuu

CARS AND BICYCLES

Be warned that petrol is expensive in Finland. There are petrol stations throughout the country but in isolated regions, and especially in Lapland, remember to check your petrol gauge often as petrol stations are few and far between. It is very common that Finnish petrol stations have cafés or restaurants where meals or snacks are served at reasonable rates until very late. True to the Finnish trait of everything being modern, petrol pumps are automatic. You make payment by inserting your bank note or credit card straight into the pump. First you need to insert your mode of payment, then press *setelikuittaus*, choose the right pump, the right petrol type and fill the tank up!

You don't need an international driver's licence in Finland. You only need your home country's licence. The Finnish National Motoring Organisation, Autolitto, is at Hämeentie 105A, 00550 Helsinki (Tel: 09–774 761).

This may be a sweeping statement, but Finland seems completely empty of traffic. One of my French colleagues says it's the only place on Earth where she sees pedestrians waiting at the side of clear roads for red lights to change to green, so that they can cross. Although the roads may be clear, and you may be tempted to take short cuts, traffic laws are strictly enforced. In fact, the government receives hundreds of millions of markkaa annually as income from traffic offences alone. The wearing of seat belts is compulsory for all passengers in a car, when driving outside urban areas and on rural roads. It is also compulsory to have your headlights turned on. Failure to comply with these simple rules means you will have to pay a fine. Drink driving is an absolute taboo; the blood alcohol limit is 0.05%. There is a great social stigma attached to drink driving.

The Finns drive on the right-hand side of the road. Most Finnish roads are two lanes wide, and the speed limit is variable, depending on whether it is summer or winter. Generally the speed limit is 50 km per hour in built-up areas; on motorways the summer limit is 100 km per hour, and in the winter it is reduced to 80 km per hour. There are two classes of roads: first-class (*valtatie*) and second-class (*kantatie*). The motorways or stretches of bypass around large towns are called *moottoritie*. The highways between major cities bear the prefix E, followed by one or two digits. Trunk roads have numbers but there are many smaller roads with no numbers at all!

As Finland is a bilingual country, many street signs are in both languages. Finnish comes first, followed by Swedish. If the local area is mostly Swedish-speaking, the signs used for places, hotels, restaurants and things to see will be in Swedish. The province of Åland is totally Swedish-speaking and little Finnish is used there.

Things to take note of when driving in Finland are as follows:

- There are no stop signs to regulate the traffic flow. This tends to cause a lot of confusion for foreign drivers. The rule is that cars entering an intersection from the right always have the right of way, whether they are on a major or minor road.

- If you spot a reindeer, slow down! This is not a joke. Truly, moose and reindeer can make motoring very hazardous. These animals don't respond to car horns and, as I once read, they feel they deserve the right of way! Whatever direction the animal seems to be heading in, move slowly, as they might just come towards you. About 4,000 reindeer are killed each year by cars, and it is a legal requirement to notify the police about any incidents involving moose or reindeer. There may be legal implications if you do not. There are two seasons in the year which seem to be particularly bad for reindeer related accidents. These are November/December and July/August. It is hardly surprising that the vast majority of accidents happen near tourist centres.

- Another thing to be aware of is that it is compulsory from 1 November to the first Sunday after Easter, to have winter tyres on your car. There are two types of winter tyres. The first is a standard snow tyre, and the second is a snow tyre which has tiny metal spikes stuck into the rubber. It is illegal to drive with tyre chains in Finland. It is the spiked tyres that allow Finnish drivers to motor along as though they were on some sort of rally, even in the middle of winter on very icy, slippery roads. The Finns generally tend to be good drivers, but your first impression is that they drive like the Italians. Distances between destinations are shorter during the winter months—I'm not kidding! Being extremely efficient, the Finns mark out official roads across the frozen lakes for traffic. Hence, instead of having to spend a large part of your journey driving around lakes as in the summer, you just make a beeline for the far shore. This is not as dangerous as you may think. The ice is very thick—thick enough to take trucks. Roadways are clearly marked and regularly checked for safety.

Cycling is extremely popular in Finland. There is very little traffic on the roads, and the country is fairly flat, making Finland a haven for cyclists. Bicycles are allowed on all public roads, except motorways. There is a very good network of bicycle paths in and around most major cities. Due to the vast distances in Finland, buses and trains are very bicycle-friendly, so you are allowed to take your bicycle on either mode of transport. And many people frequently do.

Apart from red lights at crossings, it seems to me that pedestrians and bicycles generally have the right of way. Although this may not be entirely true, it is certainly in the culture of the nation that if a pedestrian or a cyclist is knocked over by a car, it has to be the car driver's fault.

HOTELS AND LODGINGS
It is difficult to make comparisons of Finnish hotels using international star ratings. Star ratings have to be taken into context and what is one country's 4-star, may be another country's 3-star. The following comments are therefore my personal views. My observations are biased towards comparing star ratings within the UK and travelling within Europe.

There are luxury hotels, but these are few. Most hotels are geared towards catering for business people and belong to a few national chains of hotels: Scandic, Sokos and Cumulus. I would put these into a lower 3 or 4-star bracket. Generally speaking, these will have a swimming pool and saunas, restaurants and nightclubs (which may well be the most popular in the vicinity). Do be warned that Finnish hotel swimming pools are freezing! Don't do as I did on my first visit and plunge into the pool expecting to have a nice leisurely swim. The swimming pools are for people to plunge into straight from the sauna to cool themselves down. Of course, the other reason for their existence is to amuse the Finns when foreigners, like me, jump in and scream from the shock!

There is a group of independently-owned hotels called the Finlandia Group. In reality these are equivalent to 2 or 3-star accommodation elsewhere. Sometimes, first impressions may not be too good, but do not under any circumstances let this put you off. In my experience, the bedrooms are always more than adequate and, of course, being Finnish everything is immaculately clean. These hotels are modestly priced, and whilst they may not have many public facilities, they will have a restaurant. My friend Leena owns the Amado Hotel in Pori, a member of this Finlandia group, and she stakes the reputation of her hotel on the food she serves. Her restaurant has been voted the best restaurant in town for three years running and the National Sales Representatives Association has just awarded the hotel 'the Best Value for Money in Finland' accolade.

Towards the end of the summer, hotel rates are reduced quite heavily. This also applies to the weekends, Friday night through to Sunday. Breakfast in Finland is always a buffet with a selection of cheese, ham, boiled eggs, pickled fish, fresh salad vegetables, dried fruit and nuts, cereal, oats and porridge. Quite often there is a hot choice which will be a Finnish version of scrambled eggs and either meatballs or tiny cocktail-sized frankfurters. Finnish bread is tasty and varied, and the butter is delicious. In Finland, there is always a large dish of natural yoghurt and hot porridge.

My Finnish colleague Timo and I have a theory on how to judge a good hotel—by the curtains! It would seem that because Finnish windows are triple-glazed, there is no need to have thick curtains at the windows to stop heat loss as in the UK. Also, because Finland hasn't been used to having many foreigners, there is no custom of having thick curtains to shut out the light during the summer. It is still extremely common to go into a hotel room and find very thin cotton curtains at the window. Nowadays, the better hotels have recognised the need to provide more sumptuous and plush soft-furnishings. These hotels now hang heavier quality materials at the windows and behind the curtains there are metallic drapes, such as in Spain, or blinds to create total darkness.

When checking into a hotel, you will always be asked whether you want a smoking or nonsmoking room. The Finns are very fastidious about this. If you want a bath in your hotel room, you will have to request it. All rooms have showers, but very few have baths. A carpet in a hotel room is a real rarity, so it is advisable to take slippers with you. From experience, I would say that the temperature in Finnish hotel rooms is not as high as you might imagine and it is easy to get cold just sitting around. The secret of being warm in Finland is not to allow yourself to get cold. The quilts on the bed are extremely lightweight and, at first, do not seem at all cosy or warm. However, once you have warmed up and the bed has warmed up, you'll be as warm as toast.

The Finnish youth hostel associations own the majority of hostels. You will be required to bring your own sheets and pillowcases, but you can rent them if you haven't got any. Quite often there are special family-size rooms that can be rented. Breakfast will not be included in the price of the room. Guesthouses should always be inspected before you decide to stay. These tend to be in town centres and near train stations. If you are in one of Finland's old villages, you might find that the guesthouse is an old wooden house.

If you are visiting Finland during the summer, consider renting a Finnish summer cottage. This will be the best way to experience Finland. A summer cottage will normally be located near a lake, and comes supplied with the compulsory rowing boat and a sauna. Apart from that, many rental cottages come fully equipped with cooking utensils, a fridge, television and telephone. You will have to check carefully because not all of them will have electricity and running water. If you fancy experiencing the tranquillity of the countryside, these summer cottages can be booked through regional tourist offices.

Other possibilities are farmhouses, rented apartments or even wilderness huts whilst out trekking. Further information about these can be obtained from regional tourist offices.

Traditional Lappish dwellings

THE REGIONS

Lapland

Lapland is the ancestral home of the Sami people. This is the land of the midnight sun. The area covers about one-third of the total landmass of Finland and almost all of it lies within the Arctic Circle. There are large expanses of tundra, rounded hills, silent lakes, flowing rivers and some isolated birch trees. Summers are short and from October to May, snow covers the ground. Reindeer are semi-domesticated and roam freely across the land. Reindeer farming has been the traditional livelihood of the Sami. However, other Sami are now involved in the tourist or forestry industry. I am told that one of the typical traditions of the region is buying a coffee at a bar, along with a couple of hard-boiled eggs.

Reindeer farming

Karelia

Northern Karelia shares a border with Russia. The southern part of Karelia was ceded to the Soviets at the end of World War II. Thus, Karelia is regarded as a symbol of national patriotism. The Orthodox Monastery of Valamo, which was founded 800 years ago on an island in Lake Ladoga, was transferred to within the Finnish territory of Karelia where it now stands. If Lapland is the land of the midnight sun, than Karelia is the land of song. The musical instrument, 'kantele', originates from this region. The capital of the region is Joensuu. Nearby, in the Kuusamo area is the beautiful National Park of Oulanka with Koli Hill as its highest peak.

The Lake District

The main features of the central part of Finland are the thick, verdant forests and the thousands of lakes which make this part of the world unique. There are a variety and an abundance of waterways, rapids, and streams, where one can go canoeing, rafting, rapid-shooting and sailing. Some of the most stunning national parks are located in this region. Savonlinna has the beautiful Castle of Olavinlinna dating

The view from the revolving tower in Kuopio

from 1475 where one of the most famous of Finland's summer events is held, the Savonlinna Opera Festival. Kuopio is an important commercial town in this area and is located in spectacular wooded, lakeland scenery. This can be enjoyed best on an evening cruise on a restaurant boat. The best view of the town can be seen from the top of the revolving tower on Puijo Hill, which is open as a restaurant during the summer months.

Southern Finland

This is the most populated area of the country. There are many historical reminders of its past and its rich cultural diversity. Here you will find castles, fortresses, churches and historical cities, including Turku the original capital of Finland. The cathedral in Turku is the country's only medieval cathedral. It is a national shrine which has been rebuilt many times after fire and enemy attacks, and has had great significance in the formation of a Finnish identity. Rauma, a 500-year-old village near Pori, is a world heritage site. The countryside is very gentle in this part of the country.

Helsinki

The capital of Finland is Helsinki and it is sometimes referred to as the White Capital of the Baltic and the Daughter of the Baltic Sea. It is surrounded by sea and green forests and is set on a rocky promontory. It is not a great sprawling city like other capitals of the world. There are around one million inhabitants. Along with Espoo and Vantaa, Helsinki makes up the Greater Helsinki Area.

In 1812, Helsinki succeeded Turku as the capital of Finland when Tsar Alexander decided to move the capital nearer to St. Petersburg and, thus, further from Sweden. The city burnt down in 1808 and virtually all the important public buildings were destroyed. Immediate reconstruction took place, the results of which are the buildings in the centre of the town today. There are many new and modern buildings which add to Helsinki's rich variety of interesting architecture.

Suomenlinna Fortress

There are plenty of museums to visit, most notably the Kiasma Museum of Modern Art. There are some magnificent churches including one carved from rock, Temppeliaukion, and the beautiful Lutheran cathedral. Parks abound. There is the Helsinki Zoo and the Suomenlinna sea fortress to visit just off the coast of Helsinki. The Opera House, the National Theatre and Finlandia Hall all draw many visitors to their performances.

In January and February a huge church made completely of snow will stand on Senate Square. Built every year this is a major attraction.

The first day of May is a great time to visit Helsinki. The May Day celebrations will be in full swing. May Day is actually a two-day event. The partying starts the night before at six, when students ceremonially place a white student cap on the Havis Amanda statue on the edge of Market Square. The rest of the evening is then spent wandering about the town and joining in the festivities. The next morning, May Day, is a day where you have to be at the mass picnic in Kaivopuisto Park. Arrive by ten at the latest. Here you will be greeted by an extraordinary sight. The park will be crowded with happy, partying picnickers wearing white student caps. May Day has gradually evolved from a working class celebration into a spring festival for all people. Whatever the weather, the Finns will be outside in the park enjoying themselves—for this is their first day of spring.

Chapter Twelve

DOING BUSINESS IN FINLAND

Be warned—the Finns take business very, very seriously! They have been travelling and trading for centuries. Even Henry VIII, in the early 1500s, was buying tar from the Finns to make his new fleet, and Finland still has a profitable and successful shipbuilding industry.

Anyone naive enough to think that they have struck a win-win deal with a Finn, will sooner or later realise that the Finn has really got the better end of the deal. This happens, not because a Finn is trying to get the better of you, but because he is very shrewd. This fact should not be ignored, when considering the forces that shape the future of global economics. The Finns have all the attributes to become phenomenally successful in a global, commercial future. Because Finland could not hope to compete in a mass production market of consumer goods, such as Europe and the USA, they have concentrated on up-market selling. They sell quality not quantity. Their limited resources, both natural and financial, and their distance from the consumer markets, means that Finland has had to find a different way to compete in the commercial world. The attributes that have made them phenomenally successful are:

- meticulous attention to the quality of their goods
- an obsession for high technology and anything modern
- hard-working attitude
- conscientious attitude
- deep-rooted entrepreneurial and trading skills
- inbuilt honesty and ethical behaviour
- impressive language skills
- quick decision-making
- flexibility in meeting customer demands
- that pioneering spirit of trying to build up their country, such as existed in the USA in the 1800s

One Swedish businessman I know, who has worked all over the world, refers to 'Finnish efficiency' as being one of the nation's strong points. This is their ability to make decisions quickly and get on with implementation effectively. A Finnish manager is more production-orientated than people-orientated, especially when compared with his Swedish counterpart. There is always an informal relationship between the boss and the workers, and senior managers/ bosses are approachable in a way that would be impossible in southern Europe. Because the Finns are straight-talking, they can be very frank when they need to tell people when things go wrong. One Finnish managing director, with a subsidiary in Sweden, shocked his Swedish employees by telling them they had to 'pull their socks up' and become more productive. The employees could not believe they were being spoken to in such a fashion. They were not used to it. That is not the way to do things in Sweden, but it is the Finnish way!

However, there are a few traits that can let them down and stop them from realising this potential. First of all, they are very poor at marketing themselves. They won't push themselves forward. They need to get over their shyness, their reserve, and the attitude that anyone being 'pushy' is bragging. They have to come to terms with the fact that they can remain 'Honest Joe', and not lose their integrity and still communicate better with the rest of the world. Secondly, they are uncomfortable with the idea of partnerships. There still seems to be an inbuilt suspicion of sharing. Thirdly, the Finns are only just beginning to understand the concept that all customers may have different needs. The Finns value the quality of their products above all else and think that you either want to buy them, or you don't. Because of the customs and traditions in Finland, the Finns are not used to being sold to. This has a detrimental effect when they try to sell to other more 'pushy' nations of the world. Fourthly, they are not interested in making small talk and striking up relationships. As one manager said to me, "I'm there to do business. Not to find out how his wife is!" As 90% of the world's population buy on emotion and justify with fact, the Finns have a lot to learn in this respect.

I heard of a single Finnish lady who went to Hong Kong on a business trip. She felt that the trip was a disaster because her contacts spent the entire trip talking about her family, her home and her hobbies. They, on the other hand, thought she was very standoffish and uncaring because all she would do was talk about business, and never once asked them about their families! The contacts in Hong Kong were clearly trying to develop that all-important relationship before proceeding with any business, whilst the Finn was just trying to get down to business. One party was trying to build trust and rapport whilst the other party was trying to do the deal efficiently.

As Russell Snyder writes, "Although Finns are not the world's greatest experts in small talk, they are attentive and good listeners. You will find them eager to entertain you with sightseeing, a visit to the sauna, a meal in a good restaurant, an evening of drinking and dancing at a nightclub." They have a good sense of humour especially at their own expense, and they love telling jokes and exchanging business cards. They are very disappointed that the world as a whole knows very little about them, especially when they are so well-educated in geography, economy and current affairs! They will be much impressed if you can name a few of their famous athletes or racing drivers or any other facts you know about their country. Ask as many questions as you like about Finland, because the Finns enjoy talking about their country. This is the only time you will see a Finn passionate—in public, at least!

THE FINNISH HANDSHAKE

One of the most important things to remember whilst doing business with a Finn, is a good handshake. You will need to shake hands with your Finnish business colleague every time you meet, and every time you say goodbye, or until a time comes when you know each other so well that you drop the formalities. However, the important thing to note is that the Finns require you to continue shaking hands as you say your name when introducing yourself. If, like me, you are a foreigner unused to Finnish names, you may find that your handshake lasts forever. The British custom is to say your name, then extend your hand for a handshake, and shake your hand whilst saying, "How do you do." In Finland, however, you first extend your hand for a handshake, and then say your name. Sometimes, by the time you have said, "Pardon," and the person you are meeting has repeated his name, and possibly repeated it for a third time, you would have been hanging on to his hand for a long time! This really is not off-putting, as long as you know the custom. However, ladies be warned, many Finnish men have a gripping handshake, so it might be advisable to take any big rings off first! Women on the other hand, tend to have a very weak handshake.

GETTING DOWN TO BUSINESS

You will really impress a Finn by getting straight down to business after shaking hands. The Finns are very frank, direct and will tell you all that they think you ought to know to make a decision. At the same time, they expect the same of you. You will have your chance to say what you need to say and give them all the information they need to make a decision. They will rarely ask questions, believing that any information, if it were important enough, would have already been given to them.

I still remember vividly giving my first presentation to a group of Finnish business people. It is still my worst nightmare. My brief was to give a half hour presentation and allow time for questions and answers afterwards. I gave what I thought was a good and interesting presentation. I ended with a few words of Finnish, which I also had written on an overhead transparency so that everyone would understand what I was endeavouring to say. The mere fact that I had tried to speak Finnish was obviously well accepted and appreciated. However, when it came to question and answer time, I could have died. No one spoke. There was a deadly hush. The faces of my audience were very sombre. There was no spark of emotion and there didn't seem to be any interest whatsoever in asking any questions. At that moment, I felt totally lost; I didn't know what to do. It was the first time that I had ever experienced anything like this. The Finnish boss duly caught my eye, gave me a reassuring little smile, and a nod. Someone eventually asked a question, which I answered, and so the meeting ended. I was completely away from my field of experience. I had no way of perceiving whether I had done well or badly. As it turned out, I had done well and I was asked to give some more presentations. On my third presentation to some Finnish people, I paused and asked whether anybody had any questions. At that point in time, after a long pause, huge grins appeared on the faces of the audience. Someone laughed and said, "But we're Finnish." In surprise, I asked what being Finnish had to do with asking questions. Back came the reply and the enlightenment. The gentleman replied, "Oh, in Finland we don't ask questions. We give you one chance to say everything you need to say, and if it is important you will say it. Then, we will evaluate what you have said, but we don't ask questions. If we don't like what we hear, we will then go and listen to somebody else." So my initiation into doing business in Finland really did seem like a baptism of fire.

The Finns like to be viewed as specialists and experts and, believe me, the majority of them really are well qualified and well experienced in their fields. They are experts. They hate to look silly, and do not like to be shown up in front of others. They will expect you to be very well prepared, will take you at face value, but assume that you are an expert in your field. They will respect you, just as you should respect them. Remember that the Finns aren't used to being sold too. In practical terms, this means that if you begin to push your product and tell them how wonderful it is, especially if you are going through the process of an 'American sell', you will be seen to be bragging. They don't like this at all. A typical Finnish expert will be slow, calm and soft-voiced. He will know his 'stuff', and expect the quality of the products to sell the goods. However, this said, the Finns are pretty tolerant of odd people and funny habits. There is no real formality about them and they are, therefore, generally very easy to do business with. They will accept you for what you are.

When giving a company presentation, there is a vast difference between the Anglo-Saxon/American and Finnish styles. This may be of value to note. The Finns are very much into structure and facts. They like to tell you exactly where they are located in Finland, show you an organisation chart (probably with lots of names on it), give you a lot of financial details, tell you how they have grown year-on-year in figures not percentages, and generally put on screen a lot of information and numbers. They will inform you of the quality of their goods, tell you about the good design and you will learn that everything incorporates the latest technology. The purpose of their presentation is to give you information and educate you. All this will be delivered in a calm and quiet fashion. You will be given sufficient information to draw the conclusion for yourself that the product/ service is 'the best thing since sliced bread' and you can then make your decision to buy. You will rarely hear any stories, and no one promotes the benefits of using their product/service. The delivery is very factual and unemotional. Therefore, many Finns tend to find Anglo-Saxon/American-style presentations lacking in substance because of their tendency to heavily feature the benefits of buying from their company, illustrate that with stories, wring emotions and bounce around the room. Unfortunately, the nonplussed response received from a Finnish audience is usually misinterpreted by the presenter as a lack of interest, and the greater will be the effort to stir up emotion. Wrong move! Generally, the Finns are uncomfortable with emotional outbursts and are just waiting for you to give them some facts!

Letters and e-mails can be a source of confusion, irritation and misinterpretation. Because the Finns speak such good English in a one-on-one situation, there is a tendency to attribute them with having a good understanding of the way others do business. Unfortunately, written communication from them is often interpreted as commands and demands by other nationals. Again, Finnish efficiency means they do not bother to use more words than they have to and there is no 'soft' language used. They are so concerned that relevant information is understood correctly that they do not 'dress up' their correspondence. This abruptness can lead to them appearing very arrogant and unjustifiably demanding. Other nationalities can easily be offended. However, there is rarely any intention to offend.

Incidentally, an interesting thing to note is that, where the British tick boxes to indicate that something is correct, the Finns cross boxes (crosses do not mean that things are wrong). Another thing to note is that the Finns use the continental numbering system with decimal commas, not decimal points: they write 2,5 million FIM instead of 2.5 million FIM. This may seem just a small detail but I have witnessed some potentially disastrous misinterpretations! Limited companies have the initials OY (always in capital letters) at the end of their name in the same way as we use Ltd.

MEETINGS AND APPOINTMENTS

It is important to note that you should arrive at any business meeting on time. That doesn't mean to say that the Finn will always be there and ready to see you. However, punctuality is seen as a virtue, though a few minutes either way is not seen as detrimental. Office hours are generally 8:00 a.m. to 4:00 p.m., Mondays to Fridays, and business meetings might well take place from 8:30 a.m. or 9:00 a.m. Good manners would dictate that afternoon meetings should be arranged to finish by about three-thirty in the afternoon, so that people have the opportunity to make last-minute phone calls before the end of the working day.

The Finns are very hard-working; they work conscientiously and many work beyond four o'clock. It is not uncommon to find people still at their desks at five or five-thirty in the evening.

Business Hours

- Banks are open from 9:00 a.m. till 4:15 p.m. Mondays to Fridays, and closed on Saturdays.
- Post offices are open from 9:00 a.m. to 5:00 p.m. Mondays to Fridays, and closed on Saturdays.
- Office hours are 8:00 a.m. to 4:00 p.m. Mondays to Fridays.
- The majority of shops are open from 9:00 a.m. to 6:00 p.m. Mondays to Fridays, and from 9:00 a.m. to 3:00 p.m. on Saturdays.
- Larger shops, such as department stores, are found open until 8:00 p.m. Mondays to Fridays, and up to 4:00 p.m. on Saturdays.

As alcohol can only be bought in the state-owned Alko shops, it might be worth noting their opening hours: from 10:00 a.m. to 5:00 p.m. Mondays to Thursdays, and 10:00 a.m. to 6:00 p.m. on Fridays. From September to May, they open from 10:00 a.m. to 12 noon on Saturdays.

DECISIONS AND ACTIONS

The Finns come to decisions quickly, although there may well be more than one person involved in the decision-making process. Unlike in the rest of Scandinavia, they certainly do not make decisions through committees. Once they have all the facts, a decision is made quickly and then any action needed is taken immediately. In my experience, the Finns become quite intolerant of the way the rest of Europe make decisions and get to action. They cannot understand why it takes others so long; they are far more spontaneous. If you are doing business with the Finns it is important to note that you should be ready to implement any promises or any deals as soon as they are made. This will be their measure of your integrity as a business person.

CUSTOMER CARE

It is important to understand that the Finns will only give minimal information to any question you ask. This causes Finns to appear abrupt, rude, grumpy and uncaring, and does not help the impression that foreigners get of their service.

This being the case, it is important to get the question right in the first place. For example, I was at Helsinki Airport being served at the Finnair counter for international flights when two Japanese ladies approached and asked, "Is there a bank?" Without looking at the two ladies, the Finnish receptionist said, "No. Not on this side." The abruptness of the answer caused the Japanese ladies to stop in their tracks. They clearly expected an additional response. When that was not forthcoming, they eventually moved away. When I had been served, I sought out the two ladies and asked whether they were looking for somewhere to change money or an actual bank. Of course, they were looking for a *bureau de change* and I explained where it was. There are two points to consider here. First, the Finn answered the question and no more. It is not in the Finns' culture to expand upon the obvious. They do not investigate to find out what the customer really wants, or look beyond the question to see what the problem is or the question should be, and there is no responsibility to find a solution. Going beyond the call of duty is just not expected of them in their environment.

The second point to consider is the lack of eye contact. Eye contact, especially with strangers, is kept to a minimum. One Australian I met on his first visit to Finland was virtually pulling his hair out at the treatment he was getting from a girl behind the airline counter. She was clearly telling him that he could not board the plane but kept averting her eyes from his. Whatever he said, she just repeated the same message, and continued averting her eyes. He was becoming very agitated and in desperation turned to the whole audience exclaiming, "It's almost as though I weren't here. Why won't you look at me?" It was obvious the girl behind the airline counter was getting distressed. After all, she was used to the Finns obeying the rules and just going away and not making a fuss.

Another similar incident I witnessed happened to an Englishman in a supermarket. At the cashier's he asked whether the shop took Visa. The answer came back, "No." Unfortunately, the rest of the customers in the queue then had to wait at the till until the man found enough cash to pay for his items. Actually, the shop took other forms of credit cards and debit cards but not Visa. If the girl behind the counter could not speak English well, she could have pointed out the symbols/logos of the cards they took. But whether she spoke English or not, she was not going to go beyond the obvious question. Her responsibility ended with the answer, "No."

One evening, my Finnish colleague Timo and I were dining out. We both wanted just a light evening meal and decided to stop at a branch of a restaurant chain. He just wanted a plain omelette and ordered it from the waitress, who showed some anxiety about this. After some time, she returned to say that they were unable to cook an omelette because it was not on the menu. We left.

One of my clients travels the world as Customer Service Manager for a Finnish-owned multinational company. He says he is appalled at the service levels in his country and is often making comparisons with the Far East and the USA. He exclaims, "We put up with anything. We never complain!" He believes that the quality in Finland is perfect but they can't organise service, whilst in Asia they can organise service but the quality is dreadful.

PAYMENT TERMS

The world would be a better place if we could all deal with the Finns. If you send them an invoice which says payment within seven days, you will have your money within seven days. They are prompt payers, and always pay to terms. Okay—so there may be a few exceptions.

They are very naive when it comes to understanding that the rest of the world does not operate in such an honourable way as they do. They are not used to having to chase money and, as they are not used to complaining in their everyday lives, some nationals really do take the Finns for a ride—but only once.

Although most deals will be signed and sealed officially, you will never need to doubt the word of a Finn. A handshake will seal the deal. The Finns are honest and respect integrity above all else. They will not double deal you. They are frank and open and appreciate your honesty and frankness. You need not fear laying your cards on the table. But just be aware that they are good and hard negotiators.

CORRUPTION

As previously stated, honesty and integrity are high on the list of Finnish attributes, therefore, corruption is rare. If there is ever the slightest hint of corruption or bribery in government, there will be wide publicity in the daily papers. The Finnish find it difficult to deal with some foreign nations, when everyone in the chain expects to have a 'bung' (a financial payment for their effort). If they had a choice, they would prefer to walk away from these deals. They regard the whole concept as totally dishonest.

In everyday life, there is no tipping. Tipping is not in the Finnish culture at all. You do not need to tip taxi drivers, waiters or hairdressers. Even the hotel porter does not expect to be tipped. Please do not feel that you are doing them a favour by leaving them a few 'odd coppers' on the side. They genuinely take it as an insult. This is because, in an egalitarian society, everyone respects people for the jobs that they do. If their job is to drive a taxi, this is what they are paid to do, and to be civil and polite whilst doing their job is what is expected. They do not need to be tipped, and do not expect it. However some Finns, you will notice, will pay a bill by rounding up the money by a couple of FIMs (about US$0.15) and will not expect the change.

MONEY AND BANKING

There is no restriction on the import of either Finnish or foreign currency. Foreigners cannot take out of the country more than 10,000 FIM (US$1,500) unless they can prove that they brought that in. It is therefore advisable for any foreigner to declare any substantial amounts of money that they are bringing into the country.

The unit of currency is the Finnish mark. This is shortened to FIM on a sales ticket, and is usually spoken about as 'Fin Marks'. In Finnish, the unit is the markka (plural markkaa); notes come in 20, 50, 100, 500 and 1000 markkaa denominations. 100 penniä are equal to 1 markka.

Finns conduct most of their banking transactions using ATMs (cash machines) and BACs (electronic funds transfers). Finland is number one in the world for electronic banking services and the customers of Merita-Nordbanken Bank currently use over 2.8 million codewords a month when registering on e-banking. This trend is rising steadily. Internet banking is becoming extremely popular and now less than 6% of bills are paid at bank counters, 37% are paid through computers provided in the bank for customers, and a growing percentage (currently 32%) are paid through their Internet banking service. Merita-Nordbanken is developing its services to embrace WAP phones and the next generation of technology and appliances. They believe that e-banking will soon be as easily conducted on a mobile phone as on a PC terminal.

Banks have limited opening times and are not open on Saturdays. There are ATMs on nearly every street corner and in the smallest of villages. Finnish ATMs accept foreign bankcards with the symbols Visa, Eurocard, Plus Cirrus and EU. Credit and debit cards are used almost everywhere for everything, even in taxis. The need for cash here is much smaller than in Britain and elsewhere in Europe.

Chapter Thirteen

THINGS TO DO

MUSIC

Finland has a well-established music culture. From an international perspective, Sibelius, who was Finland's greatest composer, is synonymous with the musical identity of Finland and dominates this culture. Much of his work was written to glorify his own people and culture, and one of his most famous compositions, *Finlandia*, became a strong expression of Finnish patriotism and pride. Sibelius wrote his music during the time that Finland was a grand duchy of Russia and his music was seen as the rallying call to defy the giant oppressor. Today, there is a Sibelius Academy in Helsinki, which has an international reputation for turning out many fine young composers, conductors and musicians. There is also a Sibelius Museum and a Sibelius Park.

The true richness of the musical life and traditions of Finland is witnessed through the thirteen professional orchestras, eighteen semi-professional orchestras and the many ensembles in the country. Helsinki has two Finnish radio symphony orchestras and the Helsinki Philharmonic Orchestra. There are also opera and ballet companies, and solo performers, many with international reputations. For a country with such a small population, there is a remarkable number of world-class conductors, composers and performers covering a great range of artistic skills.

Good classical concerts can be heard in many towns during the summer. These are held in churches or in outdoor venues. Most are free, and are extremely popular. Helsinki has a lively all-year-round jazz scene. In the rest of the country, the jazz and rock scene takes off during the summer. There are numerous open-air concerts in parks featuring, as they say, the best and worst of Finnish music. The summer festivals attract acts from all over the world. The most famous jazz festivals are held in Pori, Tampere, and Espoo in June. Just north of Helsinki in Järvenpää, the Puisto Blues Festival is held. The best of the rock festivals can be experienced at Kuusrock in Oulu and Saapasjalkarock in Pihtipudas. Some festivals attract about 25,000 visitors. The Provinssirock Festival in June, in Seinajoki, has three stages and has attracted such stars as Bob Dylan, Billy Idol and R.E.M. (Finland has little or no drug problems.)

One of the most internationally-acclaimed festivals in Finland is the annual dance and music festival held in Kuopio which attracts performers from all over the world. One of the great opera attractions of the year is the Savonlinna opera festival. This is held in a courtyard of a medieval castle, and with world class performers, it is an experience never to be forgotten. Finland also has a wealth of modern operas that have been successfully performed all over the world.

Traditional Finnish folk music blends elements of both eastern and western culture. In fact, Karelian type folk music is a popular alternative to pop and rock. Traditional music features a combination

155

of violins, clarinets, accordions and the Finnish national instrument called a kantele.

Music is in the heart and the core of the Finnish people, and it is surprising that they have not managed to come any higher than sixth in any Eurovision song contest.

DANCING

The Finns love to dance; many of them do ballroom dances superbly. Every city and town has its dance restaurants where patrons do the waltz, tango, humppa, jenkka and the foxtrot. These restaurants engage small orchestras that play evergreen tunes. Local hotels have their dance evenings too, the most popular evenings for this being Wednesdays, Fridays and Saturdays. The midweek dance is usually advertised as *Naistentanssit*. This is the 'ladies excuse me' dance evening. If a woman asks a man to dance, he should accept her offer graciously. Similarly in a dance restaurant, men should feel free to ask a lady to dance. It is considered good manners to accept the invitation. You normally have two dances, and then the gentleman will accompany the lady back to her seat.

Believe it or not, the tango has been wholeheartedly adopted by the Finnish nation. Every year, the tango festival is staged in Seinajoki. It attracts thousands of people to the venue and is televised live to thousands of viewers.

One of the things not to be missed during the summer months is a visit to an outdoor stage dance called *Lavatanssit*. This is where local singers and their bands play popular music and people dance. The noisy dance stages seem always to be situated in the middle of nowhere. Humppa is extremely popular on these occasions. It looks great fun, and appears to be a cross between very rowdy ballroom dancing and the hoe downs held in the mid-west of the USA. The instruments used for this music are usually the accordion or violin.

SPORTS

You cannot mention the Finns without using the word 'sport' in the same breath. Outdoor activities are still an enjoyable part of the Finnish way of life. As it is so much a part of their lifestyle, this may help to explain why the Finns perform particularly well in international athletics and sporting events for such a small nation. The pre-eminence of Finland in motor sports, whether it be Formula One racing, rallying, or cross-country motor-racing, is well-known and of course their current golden boy, Mika Hakkinen, is a world champion.

The Finns, as a whole nation, walk extremely quickly. In fact, they have a very different gait from anyone else I have seen. They walk as though their upper torso is completely rigid, with just arms and legs swinging at great speed. Nearly everyone walks in this manner. The newest craze is something called stick-walking—like cross-country skiing without the skis and without the snow! People go out walking with ski poles that they dig rhythmically into the ground at great speed. This type of sport takes place during the snowless months and is said to be particularly good for health.

Trekking is a popular pastime in Finland, and there are many wilderness huts and long trails established for visitors. The lakelands are an idyllic area to cruise on old ferry steamers, whilst canoes and kayaks can be rented to explore the river ways. Cycling is also a major pastime in Finland, along with sailing on the lakes or around the large coastal areas of the country. The Finns are never far away from a fishing rod, both in summer and winter. However, if you want to go fishing, you must do so with a permit. There are several different types of permits and these can be acquired from post offices or banks. However, a local permit can be bought from a fishing location by the hour or day.

The Finns are particularly enthusiastic about ice hockey. They are just as keen on this as the British are on football. The big matches are televised and the whole country comes to a standstill when these take place. The high spot of Finland's sporting year is the World

Championships in Ice Hockey and this is as much a part of the Finnish spring as the May Day celebrations. You can tell how involved the Finns are with this sport—they have created small talk around the subject! Football, during the summer months, is a very popular pastime with most towns having their own club playing in the leagues. The success of some Finnish players abroad, Jari Litmanen at Ajax and Barcelona, Jonatan Johansson at Glasgow Rangers and Charlton, and Sami Hyypia at Liverpool, for example, has created an enthusiasm for the game. You will often find some very famous international teams playing friendly matches in many parts of the country and Finland's first purpose-built football stadium has just been completed in Helsinki.

Golf is a sport which is attracting more and more attention. Although the golfing season may appear to be short in terms of other countries, it has to be said that you can play golf twenty-four hours a day. The Finns are now promoting their country as a golfers' paradise, encouraging people to play golf at midnight. For the fanatics, there is winter golf played on the frozen lakes with red balls.

Some of the activities during the winter are ice fishing, dog-sledding, reindeer safaris, snow-mobiling and snow-shoeing. Finland offers thirty-five centres for cross-country skiing and ski-trekking, and there are a few areas in the north of the country, in Lapland, for downhill skiing. Whether it is cross-country or downhill skiing that takes your fancy, most of the trails will be illuminated during winter. Kuopio and Lahti are famous for ski jumping and these areas are where their Olympic participants train.

Sport in Finland is a time-honoured tradition, and is ingrained in every child. The Finns are well aware that modern means of transport can easily suppress the instinct for physical exercise and make them lazy. Therefore they encourage Finnish schools to have a rigorous sports programme, and every individual takes a personal responsibility to keep fit.

Snow-mobiling

CINEMA

The latest releases from an international market are screened in cinemas which can be found in every city and town. Over 80% of the films are imported, and these will probably be screened in their original language with Finnish subtitles. Even the most out-of-the-way towns screen the latest films. I have managed to see some of the latest blockbusters in Finland before they are shown in the UK. Films classified with an S are for general audiences, whilst those rated K are restricted to those over the age of sixteen or eighteen. The majority of foreign films come from the USA, France, Britain and Sweden in that order.

SHOPPING

Finland is not a cheap place to shop. However, in recent times, it has become cheaper than other Scandinavian countries and visitors can find quality goods which are value for money. Many Finns take a day trip from Helsinki to Tallin, in Estonia, to pick up some real bargains. There, you can buy the same type of goods as in Finland for much less.

A display of Finnish design

Finland is famous for its glassware, pottery, woollens, furniture and other wood products, all of which are exquisitely designed. One well-known piece of glassware that is typically Finnish is the Aalto Vase designed by Alvar Aalto, one of Finland's greatest architects, and this can be bought in shops and department stores all over Finland. From Lapland come intricate jewellery and handicraft made from wood, reindeer hide, wool and metal. Lappish hand-knitted sweaters, woollen mittens and woven wall-hangings can be purchased throughout Finland. Genuine articles handmade in the true Lapp tradition by the Sami communities carry the *duodji* label.

Department stores have a good range of products, very similar to those found elsewhere in Europe. However, they do seem to have a different and varied range of clothing. You will be able to find well-known expensive off-the-peg brands but there is a fulsome range of Finnish-designed and Finnish-made clothes. The quality of these is good and the price sensible. You will not find very cheap clothing or shoes in Finland. The Finns will not put up with poor quality.

I enjoy looking around the kitchen and home furnishing departments in the stores. Finnish design is very evident in even the simplest utensils. Amazing bottle openers, innovative egg-timers, slender glasses, must-have saucepans, intricate candles and delicate paper napkins are just some of the goods which make shopping such a delightful experience.

The Finns have a wonderful range of materials on the reel for home furnishings and dressmaking. I am always so pleased to see their traditional haberdasheries, spilling over with knitting wool, buttons and hobby kits. These types of shops have met their demise in countries like the UK.

You can also find spectacular pieces of jewellery, reflecting the traditional designs of Finland. These are both unique in appearance and very striking. Some of course are costly, but those made from copper or bronze are unique and good value for money.

Chapter Fourteen

SANTA CLAUS

No book on Finland would be complete without a mention of Santa Claus because Finland is the home of Father Christmas.

The Finnish version of Father Christmas is rather different from the modern-day equivalent in the UK or the USA. Father Christmas is usually depicted as a kind, rounded, jovial, old man. However, in Finland, he is a rather peculiar-looking mischievous elf. He is certainly dressed in red, but it is more like a Lappish costume than the red and white outfit that we see on Christmas cards and in Hollywood movies.

Santa Claus lives in Lapland—and I've been to his house. Santa's village is located just outside Rovaniemi, and it is built right where the Arctic Circle begins. In fact, strung across the village is an electric cable filled with red lights marking the boundary of the Arctic Circle. You can, therefore, straddle the Arctic Circle just as you can step across the time line in England, at Greenwich.

Artic Circle lit up

Santa's village is commercialised in a Finnish sense, which means it is modestly promoted and modestly commercialised. Those who are used to theme parks in the USA, or the well-populated parts of Europe, will find visiting Santa's village a very gentle and pleasant experience. The gifts in the shops are often handmade goods crafted by the Lapps themselves. Their craftwork is unique. The designs are colourful and intricate, and not found anywhere else on Earth. Whilst in the village, do remember to go to Santa's post office and send all your young relatives and friends an official card from Santa's village. Rovaniemi is the town in Lapland to which the Concorde flies on its one-day trips to visit Santa.

There is some disagreement as to where Santa Claus actually lives. He has a rival who lives in a town called Korvatunturi, also in Finnish Lapland, and who says he is the real Santa Claus. Here, too, you will meet Father Christmas, his wife and all of Santa's helpers. And you should remember to use the post office here, as well.

It is probably worth mentioning, while on the subject of Santa Claus, that during the months of November and December, if you take Finnair flights, you will get the opportunity to commission Santa Claus to send letters from Santa's village. A couple of years ago, I sent all my step-grandchildren some letters, and they were highly delighted, because they did come from abroad, and they truly did seem to come from Santa Claus himself.

Santa Claus himself is quite remarkable. He has an incredible knowledge of foreign languages. Whilst we were queueing up to see Santa Claus, I personally heard him speak Japanese to some young Japanese visitors, French and, of course, English, to my own daughter. You can have the official Santa photograph taken. Digitally mastered and prepared within seconds, it is of course one of those treasures to keep!

In Finland, you can hire an 'official' Santa Claus, or official 'Santa Claus Helper', to come and visit the children on Christmas Eve. These men are called Tonttu. They are officially registered and licensed to act as Father Christmas, and there is a set fee for their services. I was surprised to learn that Father Christmas services are required not only at Christmas time.

Tonttu Hannu Rosberg

I remember, quite well, one day early in February. I was flying out from Helsinki airport, northbound, when I saw a gentleman turn up to check in for the flight. He was dressed in a most peculiar outfit. Later on, we shared the same airport taxi. Although his English was not too good, I learnt that he was an official Tonttu. The photograph in this chapter is one that he gave me when I told him I was writing a book and would dearly love to mention him in it. His name is Hannu Rosberg and he even has his own web-site! These Tonttu are not as quaint and old-fashioned as you may imagine. Although Tonttu Rosberg's costume was definitely old-fashioned and traditional, and the shoes he had on were handmade from reindeer hide and he carried a wooden box tied with string to keep his belongings in, he surprised me when he took a mobile phone out from the box. My illusions were shattered. I laughed and it made a very good starting point for our conversation. We both laughed—he couldn't believe that I thought he didn't live in an electronic age, and I at my own naivety.

Santa Park

Outside Rovaniemi, there is Santa Park. This is the underground theme world of Santa Claus. It is obvious that the Park does not expect to be overwhelmed by thousands of visitors at any one time. Getting on and off the bus at Santa Park is at the same bus stop. There is no queuing system at the food hall and retrieving hats and coats at the end of your visit is quite a free-for-all. On our visit, it had only just been opened.

Do not go thinking that you might be visiting another Disney World. It certainly is not like that—there is no Hollywood gloss. In fact, it seemed to me that it was meant for young children because, at that time, there was not very much to amuse older children or adults. However, it is certainly a very interesting place to visit and it gives you an idea of how the Finns think of Father Christmas. The Finns, as I mentioned before, regard Father Christmas as being a mischievous elf and, indeed, Santa Park was very much built on that impression.

Gift shops in Santa Park

CULTURAL QUIZ

SITUATION ONE

You are giving your first business presentation to a group of Finns. The presentation seems to go well and at the end of the presentation, you stop to ask if anyone has any questions. There is total silence. No one responds. Not a single question is asked. Do you...

A   Die on the spot and run out of the room, thinking you have been a disaster?

B   Patiently wait a few moments, hand out your business card, then invite people to contact you if they would like further information?

C   Repeat your question and tell them that they really must have things to ask!?

Comments

Finns are very reserved. They do not like to stand out from the crowd by speaking up. Most probably your audience were fascinated by your presentation, have lots of questions but are afraid to ask. By handing them your business card, you allow them an opportunity to call you and talk to you on a one-to-one basis about your presentation. Answer: *B*. Remember, you are not a disaster!

SITUATION TWO

You drive to a petrol station to fill your tank. You arrive at the pump, insert the nozzle into your car, squeeze the handle, but nothing happens. Do you...

A   Look pleadingly at the attendant in the garage shop?
B   Decide the stupid thing is broken and drive to another pump?
C   Remember that technology rules in Finland and you must be to blame?

Comments

Finnish petrol pumps accept payment and pump petrol all in one operation. When filling your car up, you either insert your credit card, insert cash or use your mobile phone to key in your transaction. After that, the pump will dispense the petrol (and give you back any change remaining from your cash deposit)! Answer: *C*. Technology rules in Finland.

SITUATION THREE

When visiting a Finnish person's home it is correct and polite:

A   Not to take your shoes off
B   To take your shoes off
C   To take your shoes and socks off

Comments

The Finns keep their shoes for outdoor wear and can often be seen walking around in their stockinged feet or in sandals, even at the office. Answer: *B*. You should at least offer to take your shoes off.

SITUATION FOUR

Having a sauna in a traditional Finnish way may mean...

A   You will go ice swimming (in a hole in the frozen lake), be smeared with honey, and whipped with birch twigs.

B   A relaxing snooze in the heat, modestly attired in your swim suit.

C   An opportunity to gather naked, in a warm place, to meet members of the opposite sex!

Comments

The traditional manner in which to take a sauna generally means women and men go separately. It is not customary to keep your bathing costume on in the sauna as this is thought to be unhealthy. After a short while in the sauna, a Finn will either plunge into a cold swimming pool or lake, or have a shower and then return to the sauna (even in the middle of winter). Answer: *A*. It is thought to be very therapeutic to smear yourself with honey and be lightly whipped with birch twigs in order to stimulate the blood circulation. The cold water helps this as well.

SITUATION FIVE

You are spending the weekend in Helsinki. Your Finnish friend knows you will be alone, so you are invited for coffee. How do you behave?

A   You smarten yourself up, ensure you don't arrive dead on time (the Finns work on –ish time, don't they?) and bring a small gift with you.

B   You dress up, arrive dead on time, but come empty-handed as you are only invited for coffee.

C   You don't dress up, arrive dead on time and bring the hostess a posy of flowers.

Comments

It will be rare to be asked to a dinner party; Finns usually entertain by asking people to go for coffee. Traditionally, this will be served with seven varieties of cakes/cookies. Never be late. Even if you think you will be ten minutes late, it is polite to give your host a call. The Finns dress casually, so you will want to smarten up without getting too dressy. Answer: *C*. Arrive with a posy of flowers for the invite to coffee; or for a dinner party, you should bring flowers and/or wine.

SITUATION SIX

You have gone to a summer shindig in the middle of nowhere and need to get home. You call a local taxi firm to pick you up to take you back to the city. However, you realise you probably haven't got enough cash to cover the fare. Do you...

A   Haggle and agree the fare with the taxi driver before you set off?

B   Think he is a rural peasant and will probably charge you twice as much as he would a Finn, so on arrival start to negotiate like mad?

C   Trust that he is honourable, enquire the price of the fare, ask about a discount and not worry because you can pay by credit card?

Comments

Taxis have impressive communications systems. Wherever you are in Finland, a taxi driver can enquire the cost of a journey to a specific location and a computer will give him the exact fare. Payment by credit card can be made through the remote-controlled electronic meter installed in the car. Answer *C*. Taxi drivers are trustworthy and do not expect a tip.

SITUATION SEVEN

You are in a group of twelve at dinner. You have been served, along with the people immediately around you. Should you ...

A   Start eating so that your dinner doesn't get cold.

B   Wait for everyone to be served.

C   Start eating as soon as half the people have been served.

Comments

It is normal to start eating as soon as four people at the table have been served. Answer: *A*.

SITUATION EIGHT

Drinking a toast with Finnish white wine (*koskenkorva*) usually involves...

A   Knocking the drink back in one gulp and throwing your glass into the fireplace.
B   Taking polite sips, remembering that you are drinking neat vodka!
C   Knocking the drink back in one gulp, exclaiming "*kiipis!*"

Comments

Koskenkorva is neat vodka and the Finns are proud of the fact that it can be lethal. However, when taking a toast with this Finnish white wine, knock it back in one go. Answer: *C*. *Kiipis*, pronounced 'key-piss' means 'cheers' or 'bottoms-up'!

SITUATION NINE

When having a conversation with a Finn, an excellent topic to discuss would be:

A   Past times, especially history of the war with Russia.
B   About Sweden beating Finland at ice hockey.
C   About the unbelievable success of Nokia mobile phones— good for Finland!

Comments

Whilst the Finns are very proud of not being beaten in World War II, and are very keen on sport, the perfect topic of conversation is their global dominance of the mobile phone industry! Answer: *C*. It is almost a status symbol in Finland to have the latest Nokia phone.

SITUATION TEN

You are at the airport and have been called for boarding. Everyone has their boarding ticket and, logically, has a seat on the plane. There is a large group of people huddled around the boarding gate. Do you...

A   Find the end of the queue and wait your turn to get on the plane?

B   Just push your way in where you can?

C   Remember there is no seat allocation on domestic flights, so it is everyone for themselves, and you owe it to yourself to get on the plane as soon as you can?

Comments

There is no seat allocation on domestic flights but the Finns do queue in an orderly fashion. Jumping the queue will bring you disapproving looks. Answer: *A*. In many places there is a ticketing system to ensure people are served in order—at the post office, in banks, chemists, supermarkets, and travel agencies—but not at the airport.

DO'S AND DON'TS APPENDIX

Do

- Keep your promises—the Finns keep their promises and naturally assume you will keep yours.
- Take note that Finnish people may seem very naive (they are extremely honest), but they are not gullible. If you cross them once, you have crossed them for life. They will never trust you again.
- Shake someone's hand on a deal. It is as good as signing a contract.
- Remember that the Finns dress far more casually than most Europeans do.
- Take the nearest seat to the door in the sauna if you are not used to it, so you can get out without disturbing others.
- Remember the Finns might well want to test you by keeping the sauna very hot!
- Try the local cuisine (as my Finnish friends say, "It isn't dangerous!").
- Be prepared to drink lots and lots of coffee.
- Use simple expressions and short sentences (see note below about irony).
- Remember that Finnish people have been taught from an early age that silence is golden.
- Remember that Finnish people are very unused to small talk. They aren't rude, but can sometimes come across as such.
- Bring up Santa Claus and Nokia in your conversation. The Finns are extremely proud of these two home-grown products.
- Remember that the Finns are very proud that they fought off their aggressors in World War II and remained independent and unoccupied. However, they are a little ashamed that they had to bow to the might of Russia during the fifties, sixties, and seventies.

- Appreciate what a difficult struggle Finland has had, to be its own country, and that it is still relatively young.
- Remember that Finland was virtually a closed country until it joined the EU in the early nineties.
- Make jokes about the Swedes. The Finns have a love-hate relationship with them and, traditionally, they are the butt of Finnish humour.
- Drink only one beer if you are driving. (The legal alcohol limit is 0.5%.)
- Be prepared for the cold. The temperature will drop to −30°C at least once each winter.
- Remember that winter tyres are compulsory for driving during the cold months. Even though you think the Finns drive like maniacs on icy roads, they are used to it.
- Take into account that the atmosphere in the southern part of Finland (Helsinki–Turku–Tampere–triangle) is a lot more urban than the atmosphere in the other parts of Finland.
- Remember that Finland belongs to the Euro zone and the Finnish mark will be replaced by Euros in the beginning of year 2002.
- Note that nearly all the Finns studied English for several years at school so their passive English (understanding of English) is generally a lot better than you might think. First impressions are distorted by the fact that, in the beginning, many of them find speaking English uncomfortable.
- Note that many Finns joke about themselves in self-ironic jokes in which someone shows that mistakes can happen to herself/ himself, too.
- Remember that ice-hockey is a very popular sport in Finland. Especially among males, it is quite common to discuss ice-hockey during business negotiations.
- Remember that the scale of things in Finland is smaller than in many other European countries, the population being only some five million people.

- Remember that Finns are sport fanatics. They love their great athletes from Mika Häkkinen to Jonatan Johansson (young football talent in the Premier League).
- Be aware of the strong Finnish wholesalers and their high margins. If they don't let you into the market, you won't get in!
- Remember that Finnish women are comparatively successful and powerful in business and in politics. However, Finland is still a 'macho' country in its attitude towards women.
- Take note that in Finland, although the number one in Internet connections, newspapers, magazines, and TV are still the best media to introduce new products into the local market. TV commercials, in particular, have a great impact on sales.

Don't

- Be late for meetings—give a call if you are going to be late.
- Dress too formally for business meetings (suits are a rarity in Finland).
- Forget that Finnish 'white wine' (*koskenkorva*) is actually vodka!
- Wear your swimming costume in the sauna.
- Assume that because your Finnish colleague speaks good English, your messages have been interpreted as you want them to be understood.
- Use "Would you…?", "Could you….?" etc. when asking someone to do something. Finns don't understand that this is a command!
- Take offence when the Finns speak very directly. When they ask you to do something, it can sound like a command (see above). They say what they want and they believe what you say.
- Understate or use irony in your speech. This is guaranteed to be misunderstood.
- Speak unless you have something important to contribute.
- Be concerned if strangers do not return your big smile. The Finns are not used to grinning foreigners, but they will eventually give you a quick nod.

- Think that because everyone looks miserable, they are miserable! Finnish people are unaccustomed to walking around smiling.
- Assume that silence means agreement. Usually it means the opposite—but they won't say anything because they don't want to offend you.
- Judge Finns by their dress, manners or etiquette. They have low self-confidence in this respect, being unsure of how to dress or how to behave outside their own environment. However, they are always perfectly polite and anxious to please.
- Be surprised at how much the Finns use their mobile phones. Text messaging is very popular and they are all Olympic champions at it. Also, they use their phones to operate vending machines, along with petrol pumps and the car wash.
- Tip taxi drivers, waitresses, etc.
- Define distances in terms of time—use kilometres. It is 400 km from Kuopio to Helsinki (about four hours' driving time). In the UK, we would say that we lived about two hours' away from London by train/car.
- Drive on the left in Finland.
- Mention Finland and Russia in the same breath. The Finns hate being associated with the Russians, for whom they have a great loathing and distrust.
- Be noisy in public places—and don't let your children run around screaming and shouting.
- Think that when the Finns are quiet in a conversation, they are impolite or bored—normally it is just that most of the Finns are not accustomed to small talk.
- Think that the weather is always that cold if you visit Finland in the winter. The changes between seasons are great and the temperature can vary a lot in different parts of the country.
- Cross the street against a red light. Finnish mothers teach their children to wait until the light turns green.

- Expect Finnish companies to answer business letters or faxes. Send an SMS (text message) on the mobile phone.
- Think that young Finns are as silent and shy as the older generation. The youngsters have grown up with CNN, MTV and Interrail and quite a few have spent their summers or a whole year in the UK or in the USA.

GLOSSARY

GENERAL GREETINGS AND PHRASES

English	Finnish
Good morning	*Hyvää huomenta*
How do you do?	*Paivää*
Good evening/Goodbye	*Hyvää iltaa/Näkemiïn*
Yes, No	*Kyllä, Ei*
Thank you, Hello	*Kiitos, Hei!*
Cheap, expensive	*Halpa, kallis*
Cold, warm	*Kylmä, lämmin*
More, less	*Enemmän, vähemmän*
Mr, Mrs, husband, wife	*Herra, rouva, mies, vaimo*
Woman, man, boy, girl	*Nainen, mies, poika, tyttö*
Where, there, when, who	*Missä, tuolla, millain, kuka*
I do not understand	*En ymmärrä*
How much is it?	*Paljonko se maksaa?*
I will buy it.	*Ostan sen*
Does anyone speak English?	*Puhuuko kukaan englantia?*
I come from England.	*Olen kotoisin Englannista*
One, two, three four, five	*yksi, kaksi, kolme, neljä, viisi*
Six, seven, eight	*kuusi, seitsemän, kahdeksan*
Nine, ten	*yhdeksän, kymmenen*
Twelve, fifteen	*kaksitoista, viisitoista*
Twenty, fifty	*kaksikymmentä, viisikymmentä*
Hundred, five hundred	*sata, viisi sataa*
Thousand, five thousand	*tuhat, viisi tuhatta*
Ten thousand	*kymmennen tuhatta*
Fifty thousand	*viisikymmentä tuhatta*
Hundred thousand, million	*sata tuhatta, miljoona*

At two o'clock. Tomorrow
How long do I have to wait?
Arrival time. Departure time

Kello kahdelta. Huomenna
Kauanko minun pitää odottaa?
Saapumisaika. Lähtöaika

EATING OUT

Please bring me the menu
Please bring me the bill
Receipt, extra chair
Do you have free tables?
Where is the toilet?
I would like to order
  local specialities
Bring me something good
  you have ready

Saanko ruokalistan
Saanko laskun
Kuitin, lisätuolin
Onko teilla vapaita pöytia?
Missä on WC?
Haluaisin tilata
  paikallisia ruokia
Tuokaa minulle jotain hyvää
  mitä teillä on valmiina

Restaurant, fast food
Coffee, tea, orange juice
Beer, wine, milk, water,
  vodka
Bread, cheese, butter
Salt, sugar, pepper
Ketchup, mustard
Salad, soup, vegetables
Potatoes, chips
Meat, beefsteak
Mutton, veal, pork, sausage,
  fish
Boiled, fried
Baked, grilled
Dessert, fruit
Cigarettes, ashtray

Ravintola, pikaruoka
Kahvi, tee, tuoremehu
Olut, viini, maito, vesi,
  koskenkorva
Leipä, juusto, voi
Suola, sokeri, pippuri
Ketsuppi, sinappi
Salaatti, keitto, vihannekset
Peruna, ranskalaiset perunat
Liha, pihvi
Lammas, vasikka, sika, makkara
  kala
Keitetty, paistettu
Leivottu, grillattu
Jälkiruoka, hedelmat
Savukkeet, tuhkakuppi

TRAVEL AND DIRECTIONS

Left, right, straight	*Vasen, oikea, suoraan*
Where is …?	*Missä on…?*
How far is …?	*Kuinka kaukana on …?*
Could you tell me the way to…	*Voisitteko neuvoa tien*
Town centre	*Keskusta*
Town hall	*Kaupungintalo*
Indoor market	*Kauppahalli*
Market square	*Kauppatori*
Museum	*Museo*
Art gallery	*Taide Galleria*
Theatre	*Teatteri*
Post office, railway station	*Posti, rautatieasema*
Bus station	*Linja-autosema*
Police, harbour, airport	*Poliisi, atama, lentokenttä*
Customs, passport	*Tulli, passi*
Car documents	*Autopaperit*
Car, bus, truck	*Auto, linja-auto, rekka*
Train, aeroplane	*Juna, lentokone*
Boat, ship, ferry	*Vene, laiva, lautta*
Rail, track	*Rautatie*
Hill	*Tunturi, Kukkula*
Mountain	*Vuori*
Lake	*Jarvi*
River	*Joki*
Island	*Saari*
Park	*Puisto*
Road	*Tie*
Street	*Katu*

House	*Talo*
Church	*Kirkko*
Castle	*Linna*
Town	*Kaupunki*
Village	*Kyla*

Hotel, camping site, cottage	*Hotelli, leirintäalue, mökki*
Room for one/two nights	*Huone yhdelle/kaski yotä*
For two/four persons	*Kahdelle/neljälle henkilölle*
Bathroom, shower, TV	*Kylpyhuone, suihku, TV*
Floor, room, lift, stairs	*Kerros, huone, hiss, portaat*
Guarded parking space	*Vartioitu, parkkipaikka*
Breakfast, lunch, bar	*Aamiainen, lounas, baari*

SIGNS

Entrance	*Sis äänkäynti*
Toilet	*WC*
Ladies	*Naistenhuone/naiset*
Gents	*Miestenhuone/miehet*
Arrival	*Saapuminen*
Arrivals	*Saapuvat*
Departure	*Lähtöminen*
Departures	*Lähtevät*

HEALTH

Doctor	*Lääkari*
Hospital	*Sairaala*
Accident and Emergency	*Ensiapu*
Pharmacy	*Apteekki*

Medicine	*Lääke*
Ill	*Sairas*
Sick (nausea)	*Pahoinvoiva, Huonovointinen*
Pain	*Kipu*
Headache	*Päänsärky*
Stomach ache	*Vatsakipu*
Body	*Keho*
Arm	*Käsi Vars*i
Hand	*Käsi*
Leg/Foot	*Jalka*
Neck	*Niska*
Head	*Pää*
Eyes	*Silmät*
Ears	*Korvat*
Nose	*Nenä*
Throat	*Kurkku*
Sore throat	*Kurkkukipu*
Sore	*Kipea*
Itch	*Kutina*
Rash	*Ihottuma*
Spots	*Näppylät*
Skin	*Iho*
Sunburn	*Auringossa Palanut*
Wound	*Vamma*
Cut	*Haava*
Stitches	*Tikit*
Plaster	*Kipsi*
Antiseptic (cream)	*Antiseptinen (voide)*
Disinfectant	*Desinfiointiaine*

BUSINESS

Meeting	*Kokous*
Appointment	*Tapaaminen*

Contract	*Sopimus*
Negotiation	*Neuvottelu*
At what time?	*Mihin aikaan?*
	Milloin?
	Koska?
Turnover	*Liikevaihto*
Profit	*Voitto*
Bank	*Pankki*
Post Office	*Posti*
Headquarters	*Pääkonttori*
Owner/manager	*Omistaja/Johtaja*
Managing Director	*Toimitusjohtaja*
Finance Director	*Talousjohtaja*
Phone	*Puhelin*
Mobile phone	*Kännykkä*
Address	*Osoite*
Tel. Number	*Puhelin-numero*
Contact	*Yhteyshenkilo*
Name	*Nimi*
Expensive	*Kallis*
Cheap	*Halpa*
Value for money	*Vastinetta Rahoille*
How much?	*Kuinka Paljon?*
How many?	*Monta?*
Good quality	*Hyvä Laatu*
Reliable	*Luotettava*
Supplier	*Toimittaja*
Customer	*Asiakas*
Manufacturer	*Valmistaja*
Wholesaler	*Tukkumyyjä*

CALENDAR OF FESTIVALS AND HOLIDAYS

Public holidays

New Year's Day	1 January
Epiphany	6 January
Good Friday	March/April
Easter Sunday & Monday	March/April
May Day	1 May
Ascension Day	May
Whitsun	May/June
Midsummer	3rd weekend June
All Saints' Day	November
Independence Day	6 December
Christmas Eve & Day	24-25 December
Boxing Day	26 December

Flag-raising days

Runeberg's Day (famous poet and writer)	5 February
Kalevala's Day (national epic of Finland)	28 February
Mikael Agricola's Day (father of the Finnish language)	9 April
Veteran's Day	27 April
May Day	1 May
Snellman's Day (father of the Finnish currency)	12 May
Mother's Day	May
Remembrance Day	20 May
Finnish Defence Forces/Military Day	4 June
Finnish Flag's Day	23 June

Eino Leino's Day	6 July
(famous Finnish poet and writer)	
Aleksis Kivi's Day	10 October
(famous Finnish writer)	
United Nation's Day	24 October
Swedish Day	6 November
Father's Day	November
Independence Day	6 December

Special events in and around Helsinki

Snow Church, built in Senate Square	February-March
Sailing Season Opening	early May
Midsummer at Seurasaar	June
(midsummer festival with bonfires)	
Provincial Event, Senate Square	June
Helsinki Day	June
Open-Air Dancing (weekly)	July
Storyville Live Jazz Club (live jazz)	July
Finnish Championship League (football)	July
FeStadi (jazz, world and tango music)	July
Culinary Summer Concerts	July
on Suomenlina Island	
Helsinki City Marathon	August
Vantaa Baroque Week	early August
Helsinki Festival	end August-September
(festival of dance, music, theatre)	
Baltic Herring Market	October
Forces of Light (illumination of the city)	November–December
New Year's Eve on Senate Square	31 December

For up-to-date information on events in Helsinki and in Finland, visit:

www.helsinkihappens.com   www.hel.fi/ tourism
www.festivals.fi   www.kulttuuri.net
www.tapahtumat.net

RESOURCE GUIDE

EMERGENCIES AND HEALTH

Police: 112
Ambulance: 112
Fire: 112
24-hour health advice line: 10 023
Information about health care available around the clock. Doctors prepared to do house calls can also be contacted through this number.
Emergencies: Helsinki University Central Hospital.
Tooloo Hospital for serious accidents at Topeliuksenkatu 5, tel: 4711 and **Meilahti Hospital** for medicine and surgery at Haartmaninkatu 4, tel: 4711. Contact details for other hospitals and health centres are available in every hotel.
Pharmacy: look for the sign 'Apteekki'. Yliopiston Apteekki at Mannerheimintie 96 is open 24 hours a day.
Emergency Dental Care: Tel: 709 6611, Ympyratalo Dental Clinic at Silitasaarenkatu 18a.

All hospitals have doctors on duty around the clock. In emergencies, patients should be directed to a health centre or a hospital emergency unit. Otherwise, patients are required to present a doctor's referral and, normally, also a written statement confirming that they will pay the hospital bill. Before leaving for Finland, travellers should enquire from the health authorities in their own country whether there is a social security agreement with Finland that includes sickness benefit during a temporary stay and, if so, what the procedure is for obtaining compensation. If the traveller comes from a country with which Finland has a bilateral or multilateral agreement with provision for urgent medical care during a temporary stay, and he or she can prove entitlement to treatment as required in the agreement, he or she will be liable for the same charges as persons resident in Finland. (United Kingdom is one of the relevant countries listed.) The following documents are accepted as proof of entitlement to treatment: Sickness Insurance Card, Passport or form E111 for those who are from the UK.

LOST PROPERTY OFFICE
Tel: 189 3180. Mondays to Fridays, 8:00 a.m. to 4:15 p.m.

MONEY
Currency
The national currency is the markka (plural markkaa; abbreviation FIM). FIM1 = 100 penniä. Notes come in denominations of FIM1000, 500, 100 and 20. Coins are in denominations of FIM10, 5, 1, and also 50 and 10 penniä.

Currency Exchange
Bureaux de Change are available at the airport, the main post office, high street banks or Forex offices. An automatic exchange machine is located at the airport. Commission rates vary from 1% to 2.5%. Travellers cheques, American Express and Thomas Cook cheques are widely accepted. Some banks charge as much as FIM40 per transaction to exchange travellers cheques, while independent facilities such as Forex charge FIM10 per cheque.

Banks
Standard banking hours are 9:15 a.m. to 4:15 p.m., Mondays to Fridays. Banking machines, ATMs (Ecco), are all conveniently located.

Credit and Debit Cards

These are widely accepted, more so than in most of Europe. Use to pay for taxis and snacks instead of cash.

The Euro:

On 1 January 1999, the Euro became the official currency of Finland and ten other EU member states. The Euro is currently only used as 'written money' (cheques, bank transactions, credit cards, etc). The first Euro coins and notes will be introduced in January 2002; the Finnish markka will still be in circulation until 1 July 2002 when it will be replaced by the Euro. Euro conversion rate (fixed): 1 Euro = FIM5.94573.

ENTERTAINMENT & LEISURE IN HELSINKI

Helsinki Expert Sightseeing—Sightseeing trip aboard deluxe coach showing you the top sights of the capital. Voice-overs in ten languages and information given in small, easily absorbable chunks.

Korkeasaari—Helsinki Zoo is located on the picturesque island of Korkeasaari. Ferries from the Market Square and Hakaniemi.

Senate Square—Surrounded by neoclassic buildings, the Square represents the soul of the city. Here you can find the newly-restored grand Cathedral.

Sibelius Monument—Created in honour of Finland's most famous composer and designed by Eija Hiltunen. Set in beautiful parkland.

Temppeliaukio Church—This church has been carved inside a solid rock face and has rough granite walls and a rolled copper roof. It represents its own work of art. Go here to listen to many concerts held throughout the year.

Upenski Cathedral—This impressive, redbrick structure with 13 golden cupolas is located near the harbour. It is the largest Orthodox church in Western Europe. A must is to see the interior which is vividly and ornately decorated with exquisite icons, paintings and chandeliers.

Museums

Ateneum—The Finnish National Gallery is the oldest art museum in Finland.

Finnish Museum of Natural History—Look for the moose standing at the entrance. Fascinating collection of skeletons and fossils of mammals, reptiles, birds. Hands-on displays for children.

Kiasma—The Museum of Contemporary Art is housed in a fascinating building designed by world famous architect Steven Holl. The Museum is famed as much for its building and the aesthetic qualities of the interior design as for its contents. Café Kiasma on the ground floor is worth a visit.

National Museum—Set in a castle-style building, the National Museum houses an interesting collection of Finnish history from prehistoric to modern times.

Seurasaari Open-Air Museum—Large, spacious outdoor museum with folk buildings from different parts of Finland dating back to seventeenth century. Showing traditional rural life, also great for walks, picnics, even swimming at one or two beaches. Open May till end September.

Sports Museum of Finland—Located in the Olympic Stadium, specialising in Finnish sport and physical culture. History of Olympic Games and memories of the champions.

Suomelinna Island Fortress—This is included in UNESCO's World Heritage Sites. It is an ancient sea fortress and is the largest in Scandinavia. Still inhabited, and serviced by ferries from Market Square (Helsinki harbour), the island is both picturesque and awesome. Museum, visitor centre, church and cafés to visit. Great walks, caves, cliffs, and beach (of sorts), comes complete with canons!

Markets

Hakaniemi Market—In striking contrast to Market Square, this market is located in the heart of working-class Helsinki. Colourful stalls and an abundance of fresh produce.

Hietalahti Flea Market—From junk to gems, the best place to find anything! Fresh produce, flowers and refreshments.

Market Square and Old Market Hall—Bordered by the harbour, Market Square is surrounded by interesting and picturesque examples of architecture. Market Hall, which is located nearby, is a quaint old building and the purchase of local delicacies is a must! Sells everything from flowers to Lapp hunting knives.

VR Flea Market—Located behind the main Post Office in the old rail yard, this is the city's biggest and most popular flea market. Every square inch of platform space and wall is filled, brimming over with everything imaginable.

Beaches

Hietaniemi—Sometimes referred to locally as Hietsu, is the most obvious choice for the inhabitants of Helsinki. Swimming, sun worshipping, and modest refreshments. Bad parking, so walking or taking the bus is advisable.

Pihlajasaari—The perfect escape. Until recently, Helsinki's best-kept secret. Nice beachfront. Lots of sand, plenty of trees, rocks, boats and refreshments.

Uunisaari— A small island located five minutes by boat from the shores of the town. Boats from the Kompassi pier on Merisatamaranta. Café/restaurant, terrace, even a sauna. Must be pre-booked.

Pools

Makelanrinne Swimming Centre—This is Finland's newest swimming centre. Has Olympic-sized pool, diving tower, kiddy pools, whirlpools, sauna, steam sauna, solarium, and a gym.

Swimming Stadium—Popular outdoor pool (Olympic proportions) set in expansive grounds. Open May to end September.

Itakeskus Swimming Hall—A tropical oasis features several pools, 7 saunas, massage, solarium and gym. Situated entirely underground.

Shopping

Department Stores—Stockmann is the biggest and perhaps the most exclusive in the Nordic countries; **Sokos** is a comprehensive store which has just been completely renovated; **Anttila Kodin Ykkonen** offers a wide selection of household goods and home furnishings.

Shopping Centres—Forum is the biggest and most varied in the city centre; **Itakeskus** is 10 minutes' away by metro from the city centre and the largest shopping centre in the Nordic countries, with 190 shops, restaurants and other services; **Kluuvi** has around 30 shops and restaurants; **Kamp Gallery** has around 50 shops and restaurants, features elegant shopping gallery on three floors; **The Kiseleff Bazaar** is a treasure trove for tourists, full of Finnish handicraft, giftware and fashion. Located on Senate Square.

Bookstores—Academic Bookstore is Helsinki's largest bookstore (part of Stockmann's); **Yliopistokirjakauppa** academic books; **Meteori Books and Café** is one of the city's best speciality bookstores combined with coffee shop.

Music—Fuga for classical; **Digelius** for jazz, world, ethno; **Free Record Shop** for various music.

Clothing Stores—Marimekko; Stockmann One Way; Union Five; KappAhl; H & M; Spirit Store; Benetton; Jack and Jones; Part Two; Hugo Boss; Kuusinen.

Interesting Shopping Streets—Fredrikinkatu, Korkeavuorenkatu and **Iso Roobertinkatu** all near the main shopping area, having numerous and varied small shops with a character of their own.

The Arts, Theatres and Cinemas

Finnish National Opera—Opera and Ballet, Helsinginkatu 58, tel: 40302211

National Theatre— The biggest and oldest Finnish-language theatre in Finland. Four stages, offering about 20 plays, including children's theatre. Performances in Finnish. Railway Square, tel: 1733 1331

Helsinki City Theatre—Drama, music theatre and dance theatre. Elaintarhantie 5, tel: 394 0422

Swedish Theatre—Performances in Swedish. Erottaja, tel: 6162 1411.

Dance Theatre Hurjaruuth—Cable Factory, Tallberginkatu 1 A, 2nd floor, tel: 6931 227

Zodiak—The Centre for New Dance—Cable Factory, Tallberginkatu 1 B, tel: 694 4948

Cinemas—Information about films showing is available from hotels, daily papers and cinemas. Box offices open 30 minutes to 1 hour before the first showing of the day. Films are shown in their original language, with subtitles in Finnish.

Kinopalatsi (10 screens), Kaisaniemenkatu 2 B, tel: 0600 944 44; or **Tennispalatsi** (14 screens), Salomonkatu 15, tel: 0600 007 007.

Restaurants

This guide is extracted from *Helsinki Happens* a free English-language magazine for visitors to Helsinki (www.helsinkihappens.com).

Fine Dining

Chez Dominique—A highly imaginative French-Scandinavian gourmet restaurant with attention to season and detail, tel: 612 7393.

G.W. Sundman's—The former sea captain's house has an experimental spirit of Scandinavian flavours, tel: 622 6410.

George—A comfy classical restaurant with international gourmet dishes exploiting the best of fresh Finnish produce, tel: 647 662.

Kaarlen Kruunu—A gastronomic delight, serving from an open-plan kitchen, tel: 622 4133

Kanavaranta—Located in an old red-brick warehouse, this restaurant offers historic atmosphere with quality taste and good service, tel: 622 2633.

Kamp Restaurant—Pricey yet excellent international flavours and broad selection of wines in a glorious, thoroughly restored interior.
Savoy—Has the reputation of having the best price-quality ration of all the finer restaurants in the city. The marvellous dining room is one of Alvar Aalto's most celebrated designs, tel: 176 571.
Sipuli—Exceptional quality international cooking, broad selection of fine wines, tel: 179 9000.

Ethnic Eateries

Antiokia Atabar—Tasty Turkish flavours and belly dancing on weekend nights, tel: 6940 367.
Namaskaar—One of the first truly ethnic restaurants in Finland, still has the reputation for serving the best Indian cuisine in town. Pricey yet delicious, tel: 477 1960.
Saslik—The romantic atmosphere of Tsarist Russia offering many Russian specialities and delicacies. Russian troubadours nightly, tel: 7425 55.
Maithai—Traditional Thai food in the Far Eastern venue has plenty of vegetarian dishes. Reservations recommended at weekends, tel: 685 6850.
Mexicana—A small, cosy restaurant with full-flavoured spicy dishes and Latin American ethos. Good lunches, tel: 666 797.
Lotus—Oriental atmosphere with tasty Chinese dishes at reasonable prices, tel: 605 167.
La Petite Maison—Cosy, modest interior serving classic French cuisine with appropriate wine, tel: 260 9680.

Cafés

The Finns' enormous appetite for coffee means that a café culture is alive and thriving in Helsinki. Opened in 1861, one of the most reputed cafés is also its oldest, **Café Ekberg**, Boulevardi 9. Its pastries are the most revered in town. Try korvapuusti, the traditional Helsinki sweet roll loaded with sugar and cinnamon, at **Café Success**,

Korkeavuorenkatu 2. Choose from over 100 coffees at **Robert's Coffee Garden,** Kanavakatu 5, which is a 'gourmet roastery' which freshly roasts and grinds coffee beans on the spot. To step back in time to a more refined atmosphere, try the **Tamminiementie Kahvila**, Tamminiementie 8, which is set in an old manor house. Here the coffee pot is bottomless. Alternatively, sipping coffee by the seaside at **Café Ursula**, Ehrenstromintie 3 is a great way to simply watch the world go by.

Eating Out

Most Finns eat their main meal at lunchtime (12:30 p.m. to 2:30 p.m.), when restaurants (ravintola) offer special meals from about FIM35. In the evening, Finns have their dinner at home, around 6:00 p.m. to 8:00 p.m. If dining out, most will eat between 8:00 p.m. and 10:00 p.m. For more informal dining, baari and kahvila serve less expensive options. Service charge and sales tax are included in the advertised price. The main eating districts are all centrally located around or on the streets off the Esplanadi, Bulevardi and Mannerheimintie.

Finnish cuisine is traditionally a mélange of East and West, namely Russian and Swedish, and is seasonal. In the summer, many restaurants are full of fresh, locally-grown produce including the Helsinki speciality, crayfish. In the autumn, mushrooms, berries and game are on offer. Firm staples throughout the year include meat, potatoes, fish, milk, butter and rye. Salmon is one of the most popular mainstays; grilled, fried, or made in the Helsinki version of sushi (wrapped around new potatoes). It is also used in soup. Roasts, diced meat, pork chops, mince and speciality sausages are also firm favourites. Finnish dishes are traditionally covered in heavy sauces. In recent years, cooking has become far more international and restaurants will offer dishes from a wide range of countries.

TRANSPORT AND COMMUNICATIONS

Flights to Helsinki
Helsinki-Vantaa International Airport (HEL)
Tel: (09) 82771 or (09) 615 11 Fax (09) 82 77 30 99.
Web site: www.ilmailulaitos.com
The airport, with two linked terminals for national and international traffic, is located in Vantaa, 19 km (about twelve miles) from the city centre. There is no departure tax.

Major airlines: More than 25 airlines fly into Helsinki from all major European cities, including a daily service from New York, nonstop flights from Miami, San Francisco and Toronto, and direct flights from Singapore, Bangkok and Tokyo. The national airline is Finnair, tel: (09) 600 8100 or 818 800 or 818 8383. (London, tel: 0990 99 77 11.) There is a 24-hour automated telephone service in English. E-mail: information@finnair.fi; web site: www.finnair.fi.

Approximate flight times to Helsinki: From London, 2 hours 50 minutes; from New York, 8 hours; from Los Angeles, 17 hours 15 minutes; from Toronto, 8 hours 40 minutes; and from Sydney, 27 hours 30 minutes (with two stopovers).

Airport facilities: Duty-free shops and boutiques, restaurant, bar, R-kioski (newsagents), bureaux de change, automatic exchange machines, ATMs (bank/cash machines), travel agencies, tourist information and car hire from Avis, Budget, Europcar Interrent and Hertz.

Business facilities: There is a VIP lounge with fax and phone facilities, and a cafeteria; as well as a conference room which can be hired. Tel: (09) 818 3629.

Transport to the city: Bus 615 goes to Rautatientori (Railway Square) every 20-30 minutes (cost: FIM16); while a Finnair bus goes to the centre with various stops (cost: FIM27). Standard taxis charge FIM150, while shared taxis, run by Yellow Line, cost FIM100 (tel: (09) 106 464).

Getting Around Helsinki
Public Transport
Helsingin Kaupungin Liikennelaitos or HKL (Helsinki City Transport; tel: (09) 010 0111; web site: www.hel.fi/HKL) operates the metro, local trams, buses and the ferry to Suomenlinna Island Fortress.

Tickets: A ticket for a single journey on any type of transport costs FIM10 (when purchased on board), or FIM8 (when purchased beforehand); books of ten tickets cost FIM75. Tickets solely for trams are cheaper at FIM8 (on board) or FIM6 (pre-purchased). Transfers are allowed for single and multi-trip tickets within one hour of the time stamped on the ticket when initially boarding. Tickets can be purchased from newsagents (R-kioskis), metro stations, the City Tourist Office and the post office. Buses and trams run from 5:45 a.m. to midnight.

Passes: The Helsinki City Transport Tourist Ticket allows unlimited travel on all buses, trams, metro and local trains in Helsinki.

The Helsinki Card: A handy and economical way of getting around the city and getting to know its numerous attractions. A transport and entrance ticket all in one. The card is accompanied by a 96-page guide book. Unlimited free travel on public transport and free entrance to the major sights of Helsinki. 24 hour pass FIM 135, 48 hour FIM175, 72 hour FIM205.

Taxis: Most taxis are Mercedes. They can be hailed on the street or booked by telephone from Helsinki Taxi Centre (tel: (09) 700 700). A trip around town will cost about FIM150. A taxi is available for hire if the yellow 'TAXI' sign is lit. Tipping is not required.

Limousines: Providers include: Limousine Service Helsinki, Tuulimyllyntie 7 (tel: (09) 79 7800; fax: (09) 2797 8027). Rates are from FIM270 per hour.

Driving in the City

As the public transport system is excellent and most of central Helsinki is accessible on foot, it is not necessary to take a car into Helsinki city centre. Parking is also reasonably expensive: meters cost FIM3-12 per hour, and parking spaces cost as much as FIM10 per hour and upwards.

The city is divided into three parking zones, of which Zone I (I-vyöhyke) is the most central, and accordingly the most expensive. With a few exceptions, parking is free after 6:00 p.m. Parking meters take ordinary coins or parking cards, which can be purchased in advance from R-kioski and service stations.

Car Hire: Car hire costs from about FIM170 per day and FIM2 per kilometre. A credit card is usually required as a deposit. The minimum age for car hire varies from nineteen to twenty-one and extra charges are made for additional drivers. One year's driving experience is required. Car hire is available at the airport, railway station, major hotels and tourist offices. Operators include: Budget, Malminkatu 24 (tel: (09) 686 6500; fax: (09) 685 3350), Europcar InterRent, Radisson SAS Hesperia Hotel (tel: (09) 4780 2220, fax: (09) 4780 2222) , and Hertz, Mannerheimintie 44 (tel: 020 555 2300).

Bicycle Hire: Owing to Helsinki's flat terrain, bicycles are a popular way of getting around and the lanes run concurrently with footpaths. It should be noted that all bike traffic lights must be obeyed to avoid a fine. Pedal power options can be obtained from Cat Sport Oy, Toolonlahti kiosk on the Finlandia Hall shore (tel: 0400 404 012) and Rastila Camping, Karavaanikatu 4 (tel: (09) 321 6551). Helsinki City Transport has bikes available at 25 locations in the city centre. A

FIM10 pawn is returned after use. Information about cycling events is available from the Cycling Union of Finland, Suomen Pyöräilyunini, Radiokatu 20 (tel: (09) 278 6575, fax: (09) 278 6585).

Boat Hire: In the summer, rowing boats and kayaks are a popular way of island hopping and getting around Helsinki's shoreline. These can be hired from Cat Sport Oy, Toolonlahti kiosk on the Finlandia Hall shore (tel: 0400 404 012) and Rastila Camping, Karavaanikatu 4 (tel: (09) 321 6551).

Telephone

All public telephones accept phonecards, sold in units of FIM100, 50 and 30. Local calls take FIM10, 5 or 1 Markka coins. The minimum charge for a local call is FIM2. Cheap rates are from 9:00 p.m. to 8:00 a.m. and all day Saturday and Sunday.

Mobile Phones: Both the GSM 900 and GSM 1800 networks operate in Helsinki. Visitors from the USA and Canada should obtain a European-standard handset and an SIM card in order to make calls in Finland. All foreign visitors should consult their service provider for details of roaming agreements. Mobile phone hire is available at the airport from AIR Foto (tel: (09) 822 099; fax: (09) 822 990). Phones are hired out by the day for FIM50.

Dialling Codes:
City code: 09 (when dialling from outside Finland, the initial '0' is dropped)
Country code: 358
Outgoing international code: 990, 991 or 999
Directory enquiries (in English): 118 or 020 202
International directory enquiries: 020 222
Operator (in English): 118
International operator: 020 222

Post

The main post office in Helsinki (tel: (09) 020 4511), is located at Mannerheiminaukio 1a and is open from 9:00 a.m. to 9:00 p.m. Mondays to Fridays, 10:00 a.m. to 6:00 p.m. on Saturdays and Sundays. Facilities include *poste restante*, ATMs, telephone and fax facilities and *bureaux de change*. Postage within Finland for letters up to 50g costs FIM3.50. Postcards and letters up to 20g cost FIM2.70 to EU countries, FIM3.20 to other European countries and FIM3.40 elsewhere.

Letters within Europe will take two to four days; post to the USA, Canada and Australia may take up to two weeks.

Courier Services

Providers include TNT (tel: 0800 88800 or (09) 476 266), DHL (tel: 0800 77744 or (09) 696 9121), and World Courier (tel: (09) 8700 3300).

Internet Access

Public libraries such as Rikhardinkadun Library, Kirjakaapeli (tel: (09) 31 08 50 00; e-mail: Kirjakaapeli@ lib.hel.fi) provide free Internet access, but bookings should be made in advance. Internet cafés can also be found in central Helsinki.

MEDIA

Press

Helsingin Sanomat is the largest Finnish-language daily. English-language newspapers and journals such as the *International Herald Tribune* and *The Economist* are widely available. Free English-language listings include *Helsinki Happens* (web site: www.imagepublishing.fi/helsinkihappens), and the *Helsinki Guide*, available from the City Tourist Office.

TV and Radio

Two national channels, TV1 and TV2, as well as two commercial channels, MTV3 and Nelonen, broadcast English-language programmes from Britain and the USA; otherwise programmes are in Finnish or Swedish. There are four national radio stations (www.yle.fi/rfinland). In Helsinki, Capital FM (103.7MHz) broadcasts English programmes such as BBC World News, Voice of America and Radio Australia. BBC World Service and Voice of America frequencies are correct at the time of going to press, but do change.

BBC: MHz 17.64 12.10 9.410 6.195

Voice of America: MHz 11.97 9.760 6.040 0.792

GENERAL COUNTRY INFORMATION

Language

Finland has two official languages: Finnish and Swedish. Finnish, a Finno-Ugric language, is spoken by 93% of the population, while Swedish, mostly found in pockets on the southwest coast, is the mother tongue of 6% of Finns. In remote parts of the north, about 1700 people still speak Sami (more commonly known as Lappish).

As only five million people speak Finnish, foreign languages are a must for the Finns. English, an integral part of the school curriculum, is widely understood. A number of Finns also speak Russian and/or German. Most restaurants have menus in Finnish and English.

Helsinkiläiset (people from the Helsinki region) consider their Finnish the yardstick of cosmopolitan Finland, while regional accents are viewed as provincial. There are a number of slang words idiosyncratic to the capital, such as *dösä* (bus), *spora* or *ratikka* (tram), *bisse* (beer) and *rööki* or *spaddu* (cigarette), among others. Helsinkiläiset are proud of their Finnish language, and rather than adopt English-isms like the French (for example, *le ski, le surf*), they coin their own Finnish words to preserve their mother tongue.

Voltage, Connections and Measurements

The electric current in Finland is 220 volts, 50Hz. Plugs are European two-pin plugs. Most hotel rooms have telephone sockets for modem dialling to the Internet. The better hotels have a mobile telephone charging stand at the reception for guests, labelled for about half a dozen different makes and models of phone. Measurement is metric; and temperature is measured in centigrade.

Embassies

Address	Telephone
Argentina, Bulevardi 5 A 11	607 630
Austria, Keskuskatu 1 A	171 322
Belgium, Kalliolinnantie 5	170 412
Canada, Pohjoiseplanadi 25 B	171 141
Chile, Erottajankatu 11	612 6780
China, Vanha Kelkkamaki 9-11	228 9010
Czech Republic, Armfeltintie 14	171 169
Denmark, Keskuskatu 1 A	684 1050
Estonia, Itainen Puistotie 10	622 0288
Fed. Rep. Germany, Krogiuksentie 4 B	458 580
France, Itainen Puistotie 13	618 780
Great Britain, Itainen Puistotie 17	2286 5100
Greece, Maneesikatu 2 A 4	278 1100
Hungary, Kuusisaarenkuja 6	484 144
Iceland, Pohjoiseplanadi 27 C, 2nd floor	612 2460
India, Satamakatu 2 A 8	608 927
Ireland, Erottajankatu 7 A	646 006
Israel, Vironkatu 5 A	135 6177
Italy, Itainen Puistotie 4	681 1280
Japan, Etelaranta 8, 4th floor	686 0200
Mexico, Simonkatu 12 A, 7th floor	5860 4322
Netherlands, Erottajankatu 19 B	661 737
Norway, Rehbinderintie 17	686 0180

Poland, Armas Lindgrenin tie 21	684 8077
Portugal, Itainen Puistotie 11 B	682 4370
Russian Federation, Tehtaankatu 1 B	661 876
South Africa, Rahapajankatu 1 A 5	6860 3100
Spain, Kalliolinnantie 6	687 7080
Sweden, Pohjoisesplanadi 7 B	651 255
Switzerland, Uudenmaankatu 16 A	649 422
Turkey, Puistokatu 1 b A 3	681 1030
USA, Itainen Puistotie 14 A	171 931
Venezuela, Bulevardi 1 A 62	641 522
Yugoslavia, Kulosaarentie 36	684 7466

BUSINESS INFORMATION

Helsinki is seen as the Baltic region's commercial gateway to Sweden and Russia. It rates as one of the world's top 20 conference centres, and has played host to events such as the first USA/Soviet summit in 1990, when George Bush met Mikhail Gorbachev.

Finland has recently been rated as Europe's most competitive country by the Swiss research institute IMD, which praised it for its business practices, skills and ability to be highly adaptable in adverse circumstances. The unemployment rate became the second-highest in Europe, during the recession of the early 90s, at a staggering 20%, but is now 11%. This fall is attributed to the government cutting back on everything except education and research (one-fifth of all Finns have a university degree or equivalent). This has enabled Finland to become one of the world's leading telecommunications equipment producers, making everything from mobile phones to GSM networks. This industry now vies with the country's traditional exports of pulp and paper (each account for 40% of Finnish exports). Helsinki Technical University experts predict that within seven years, Finland's software developers will employ as many people as the forestry industry does today.

Nokia is perhaps Finland's biggest success story. It is now the second-largest manufacturer of mobile phones, forecasting sales of 600 million units within five years. The company is one of Helsinki's main international companies, along with Stora Enso, Finnair, Merita Nordbank and Leiras.

Business Etiquette

Standard office hours are 8:00 a.m. to 6:00 p.m., with a one-hour lunch break between 12 noon and 2:00 p.m. The Finns are punctual to the minute and lateness is seen as a discourtesy; they will always alert a colleague of an impending delay, even if it is a matter of minutes. German playwright Bertold Brecht is famed for saying that the "Finns are silent in two languages." They are a naturally reserved people and garrulous people are viewed with suspicion. When meeting for the first time, a handshake is customary, as is formal dress (suit and tie for men, especially in Helsinki), but the Finns are not flashy dressers and trousers and jacket are more common; dress is smart-casual and women often wear trouser suits. Business cards are vital. Meetings and business deals are often conducted by phone or in a sauna. Although these places are traditionally regarded as retreats; meetings often take place in the relaxed, less formal environment. Note that business is still very serious, even when you haven't your clothes on. The Finns are completely unabashed about going *au natural* in the sauna; although sometimes mixed, there are usually separate saunas for men and women and a towel is on hand to wrap yourself. It is rare for business acquaintances to be invited to a Finnish home to conduct business. If invited to someone's house for dinner, lateness (over 10 minutes) is seen as a discourtesy. Shoes are usually removed before entering the house; and a gift for the host, like a bottle of wine or flowers, is seen as courteous.

Useful Contacts

City of Helsinki Tourist Office
Pohjoisesplanadi 19, 00100 Helsinki
Tel: (09) 169 3757. Fax: (09) 169 3839.
E-mail: tourist.info@hel.fi
Website: www.hel.fi/tourism

Finnish Tourist Board (Helsinki)
Eteläesplanadi 4
P.O. Box 249
00131 Helsinki
Tel: + 358 (0) 9 4176 9300
Fax: + 358 (0) 9 4176 9399
Email: mek.espa@mek.fi
Opening times: October-April, 9:00 a.m. to 5:00 p.m. Mondays to
Fridays; May-September, 9:00 a.m. to 5:00 p.m. Mondays to Fridays,
and 10.00 a.m. to 2:00 p.m Saturdays and Sundays.

Finnish Tourist Board (UK)
PO Box 33213, London SW1Y 5ZS
Tel: (020) 7365 2512, (information & brochures) (020) 7930 5871
(trade and press only). Fax: (020) 7321 0696.
E-mail: finlandinfo@mek.fi (information & brochures),
mek.lon@mek.fi (trade and press only)
Website: www.finland-tourism.com

Business Services

Convention and meeting planners
Helsinki-Finland Congress Bureau
Fabiankatu 4b, 00130 Helsinki
Tel: (09) 668 9540. Fax: (09) 66 89 54 10.
E-mail: hfcb@hfcb
Website: www.hfcb.fi

Finland Travel Bureau Ltd
PO Box 319, 00101 Helsinki
Tel: (09) 18 261. Fax: (09) 622 1524
E-mail: groups.incoming@smt.fi
Website: www.smt.fi

Finland Travel Marketing
Sibeliusaukio, 004400 Järvenpää
Tel: (09) 2790 970. Fax: (09) 2712 843
E-mail: rauno.pusa@ftm.inet.fi
Website: www.finland-tm.com

Bennett BTI Nordic
Congress Service, PO Box 1149,
00101 Helsinki
Tel: (09) 685 850. Fax: (09) 68 58 52 80.
E-mail: helsinki.incoming@bennettbti.com
Website: www.bennettbti.com

Congrex Blue & White Conferences
PO Box 81, Sulkapolku 3, 00371 Helsinki
Tel: (09) 560 7500. Fax: (09) 56 07 50 20.
Website: www.congrex.com

Convenio Ltd
Ilmarinkatu 10c, 00101 Helsinki
Tel: (09) 241 0424. Fax: (09) 241 0425.
E-mail: convenio@pp.kolumbus.fi
Website: www.convenio.fi

Marina Conventure
Pajalahdentie 9, 00200 Helsinki
Tel: (09) 682 2306. Fax: (09) 682 2307
E-mail: marina@marinaconventure.fi

TSG Congress
Kaisaniemenkatu 3b, 00100 Helsinki
Tel: (09) 628 044. Fax: (09) 667 675.
E-mail: info@tsgcongress.fi

Congress and Meeting Venues
Finlandia Hall
Mannerheimintie 13e, 00100 Helsinki
Tel: (09) 40241. Fax: (09) 446 259.
E-mail: finlandiahall@fin.hel.fi
Website:http://finlandia.hel.fi
The hall is in Hesperia Park, within walking distance of the larger
hotels. It has a capacity for up to 2000 people and seating in the main
auditorium for up to 1700.

Helsinki Fair Centre
PO Box 21, 00521 Helsinki
Tel: (09) 15091. Fax: (09) 142 358.
E-mail: info@finnexpo.fi
Website: www.finnexpo.fi
The centre has several restaurants, cafés and private dining rooms,
with total seating for up to 2940.

Marina Congress Centre
Katajanokanlaituri 6, 00160 Helsinki
Tel: (09) 16 661. Fax: (09) 629 334
E-mail: grandmarina@scandic-hotels.com
Website: www.scandic-hotels.com
5 meeting rooms, 7 conference halls for 150-2000 guests. Video
monitoring system, closed-circuit TV system, teleconferencing fa-
cilities, permanent TV and radio cables for mobile broadcasting units.
Paasitorni Conference Centre

Pastorni

Paasivuorenkatu 5a, 00530 Helsinki

Tel: (09) 708 9611. Fax: (09) 708 965.

E-mail: myynti@paasitorni.fi

Website: www.paasitorni.com

This centre has large conference halls and seats up to 2000 banqueting guests.

Radisson SAS Royal Hotel Helsinki

Runeberginkatu 2, 00100 Helsinki

Tel: (09) 695 80. Fax: (09) 6958 7100

E-mail: info@helzh.rd.sas.com

Website: www.radisson.com

5 meeting rooms, 5 conference rooms for 150-1000 guests. 262 hotel rooms including 8 suites.

Strand Inter-Continental Helsinki

John Stenbergin ranta 4, 00530 Helsinki

Tel: (09) 39 351. Fax: (09) 393 5255

E-mail: strand@interconti.com

Website: www.interconti.com

4 meeting rooms, 2 conference rooms for up to 800 guests. 200 hotel rooms including 8 suites, 4 saunas, swimming pool. 24-hour room service, airline check-in.

BIBLIOGRAPHY

Asplund, A. & U. Lipponen, *The Birth of the Kalevala,* Finnish Literature Society, Helsinki, 1985.

Brewer, J. & M. Lehtipuu, *Finland,* Lonely Planet Publications, Victoria (Australia), 1999.

Dahlgren, M. & M. Nurmelin, *Sauna, Sisu and Sibelius: A Survival Guide to Finnish for Business People,* Yrityskirjat OY, Finland, 1999.

Finnair *Blue Wings Magazines* and *Finland Books* (inflight publications).

Finnish Tourist Board @ www.mek.fi/mek_page1.html.

Hautala, J., *Finnish Folklore Research 1828-1918,* Finnish Society of Sciences, Helsinki, 1968.

Honko, L, 'A Hundred Years of Finnish Folklore Research: A Reappraisal', in *Folklore,* vol. 90, no. 2, 1979.

Kirby, D.G., *Finland in the Twentieth Century,* Hurst, London, 1979.

Lönnrot, E., *The Kalevala,* translated by Kirby, Athlone Press, London, 1985.

Magoun, F.P., *The Kalevala or Poems of the Kalevala District,* Harvard University Press, Cambridge, 1985.

Nurmelin, M., *Business People,* Yrityskirjat OY, Helsinki, 1999.

Paasivirta, J., *Finland and Europe: International Crises during the Period of Autonomy, 1808-1914,* Hurst, London, 1981.

Ramnarine, T.K., 'Folklore and the Development of National Identity in Finland', *Europa,* (no.1 article 6), 1996.

Rintala, M., *Four Finns; Political Profiles: Mannerheim, Tanner, Ståhlberg, Paasikivi,* University of California Press, Berkeley, 1969.

Screen, J.E.O., 'Finland', *World Bibliographical Series,* vol. 31, Clio Press, Oxford, 1981.

Singleton, F., *A Short History of Finland,* Cambridge University Press, Cambridge, 1989.

Snyder, R., *The Lighter Side of Finland: For Businessmen,* Yrityskirjat OY, Helsinki, 1996.

Taylor-Wilkie, D., *Finland,* Insight Guides, APA Publications (HK) Ltd, 1996.

Wilson, W.A., *Folklore and Nationalism in Modern Finland,* Indiana University Press, Bloomington, 1976.

Wuorinen, J., *A History of Finland,* Columbia University Press, New York, 1965.

THE AUTHOR

Deborah Swallow is recognised as one of the finest trainers in Britain, having won the *1999 UK National Training Award,* the highest accolade in the business. She was one of the first women to be appointed to the Board of a UK Training and Enterprise Council, and was involved in the setting up of the new Small Business Service and the Learning and Skills Council.

She is a professional speaker, and a Director of the Professional Speakers Association of Europe (PSA). She speaks on business issues, from the point of view of an entrepreneur. Much of her working life is spent abroad, lecturing and training in multi-cultural matters, and guiding companies in Scandinavia and other European countries in doing business more effectively across national borders.

A successful businesswoman herself, she is currently Managing Director of two businesses and finishing a Doctorate in Change Management.

INDEX